# Covered
# non-League

More from Mike Floate's Collection of Football Ground Images as featured on the Covers of Clubs' Programmes and Other Publications

## Wested Meadow

<u>Right</u>: Programme from
Crockenhill v. Bearsted
1st October 2005

<u>Cover</u>: Programme from
Crockenhill v. Deal Town
4th April 1998

Published by Newlands Photographic,
71 Stones Cross Road,
Crockenhill, Swanley, Kent BR8 8LT

Text, concept and layout © Mike Floate 2016

ISBN SBN 978-1-900257-29-9

Printed and bound by Catford Print Centre

~ Saturday October 01st 2005 ~
Lea-Ray Senior Trophy ~ 1st Round
**Crockenhill**
Verses
**Bearsted**
Sponsored by Gladwish Land Sales
www.GLSfootball.co.uk

Official Programme £1
Crockenhill FC are Kent's Top Village Football Club

# Covered non-League

In 2015 I published *Covered*, having been collecting programmes with photos of grounds on the cover for twenty years. So many people asked when a non-League edition would be out that I reviewed the rest of my collection. With just fifty or so programmes it was not going to be immediately. One kind buyer, Eric Owens, even enclosed two Kingstonian programmes with his order for *Covered,* while both John Daniels and Phil Paine brought me a number of programmes that they found.

The programmes in this book are arranged by and large in alphabetical order. Some will be seen to be out of sequence but the need to keep clubs with two programmes featured on the same page meant that some shuffling was needed.

Ground names caused some difficulty. For example Bexley United called their ground the Welling Ground. The club had been re-named from Bexleyheath & Welling who had called it the Town Ground, and the current occupants Welling United call it Park View Road. Another club which changed their name was Wellington, playing at Buck's Head, while Telford United played at Bucks Head. Apostrophes were probably included in other ground names at one time.

Some clubs have used variations on a ground name over time so I have used the name in use at the date of the match featured. Hence Crockenhill is listed as Wested Meadow not "Wested" (with inverted commas) as found in old *Non-League Directories*.

It soon became clear that many clubs only began using photos on the covers of their programmes relatively recently, while others were featuring their ground back as early as the 1930s, before any of the programmes in *Covered* were issued. The use of aerial photos in the late 1950s and early 1960s provided me with many excellent images for League grounds, but only very few non-League clubs seemed to be able to source these.

Interestingly, in recent years many clubs have featured their grounds on their programme covers or used action photos which include part of the ground. Of course, any club using a photo of one of those dreadful portable metal seating units so easily provided by grants these days will look in vain for their programme. They won't be in here: real grounds only.

I am proud to include four Crockenhill programmes from my time as the club's programme editor. My design and layout from twenty years ago is still an influence on the club's programme today. The cover photo on this book of the 1997/8 season programme includes my late father at the only game he ever attended at Wested Meadow. He was always interested in seeing my new books and would have been proud to feature on one.

A year later the club were playing at Erith & Belvedere due to Kent League floodlight requirements. We saw that the Kent FA did not demand lights in their cup games so these were played at Wested Meadow, hence both grounds being on the cover. Needless to say the curmudgeons at the KCFA were thoroughly unimpressed and quickly changed the Senior Trophy rules.

▶

*The photo on the Hillingdon Borough cover on page 88 is an excellent example of a great photo being used. On opening the cover it is then seen to be just half of a standard landscape ground photo. Sadly the photographer is not credited.*

The 2005/6 cover photo was taken by me but on time delay. I set the timer going and ran to join the team group. Chairman Steve Cullen's two boys Ryan and Reece were also included and eleven years on are both established first team players for the club.

Finally, please don't ask me about a third volume as there won't be a *Covered Abroad* book unless someone else decides to compile and edit it!

FINAL GAME AT THE "LEAS STADIUM"

Southern League-Southern Division | Souvenir | Hillingdon v. Chatham Town
Tuesday 23rd April 1985 Kick Off 7-30pm | Programme |

50p

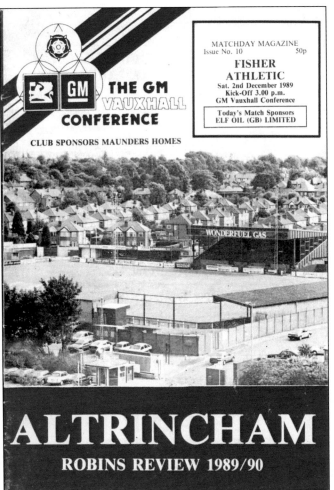

MATCHDAY MAGAZINE
Issue No. 10                    50p

**FISHER
ATHLETIC**
Sat. 2nd December 1989
Kick-Off 3.00 p.m.
GM Vauxhall Conference

Today's Match Sponsors
ELF OIL (GB) LIMITED

**THE GM
VAUXHALL
CONFERENCE**

CLUB SPONSORS MAUNDERS HOMES

WONDERFUEL GAS

**ALTRINCHAM**

ROBINS REVIEW 1989/90

◄

Programme from
Altrincham v. Fisher Athletic
2nd December 1989

►

Programme from
Altrincham v. Radcliffe Borough
16th December 1989

►►

Programme from
Accrington Stanley v. Newtown
3rd September 1988

# The Crown Ground

# THE STANLEY SCENE

### SEASON 1989/90

### PRICE 40p

## ACCRINGTON *Stanley*

### ONE OF FOOTBALL'S OLDEST NAMES

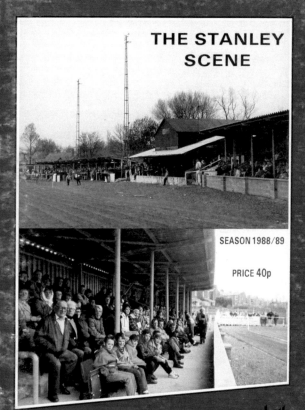

# THE STANLEY SCENE

### SEASON 1988/89

### PRICE 40p

## ACCRINGTON *Stanley*

### ONE OF FOOTBALL'S OLDEST NAMES

# Gedling Road

◄

Programme from
Arnold v. Harworth C.I.
22nd September 1987

►

Programme from
Ashford Town v. Dorchester Town
2nd May 1987

# Essella Park

►►

Programme from
Bamber Bridge v. Workington Town
11th October 1994

# Irongate

AUGUST 16, 1930
KENTISH EXPRESS.

## FOOTBALL

### ADDITIONAL KENT LEAGUE
### PROSPECTS

KENTISH EXPRESS,
AUGUST 23, 1930

## FOOTBALL

### STEP UP FOR
### EIGHT KENT
### CLUBS

Kentish Express, Thursday, April 30, 1987

## UP TOWN BOYS

Leatherhead 0, Ashford 2

# DORCHESTER TOWN

*May 2nd - 1987  Southern League South*

£1

## WELCOME TO IRONGATE

### Bamber Bridge F.C. v

Workington Town F.C.

THE NORTHERN PREMIER
FOOTBALL LEAGUE

**1994/95 SEASON**
**OFFICIAL PROGRAMME**

60p

Bob Lord Challenge Trophy 2nd. Round 2nd. Leg

WEALDSTONE

Tues. Dec. 13th. 1983
K.O. 7.30 p.m.

MATCH DAY
MAGAZINE 30p

# Underhill

◄

Programme from
Barnet v. Wealdstone
13th December 1983

►

Programme from
Barton Rovers v. Horsham
8th November 1980

# Sharpenhoe Road

►►

Programme from
Bashley v. Ashford Town
19th October 1991

# Bashley Road

## BERGER
### Isthmian League

## Division 2
## Official Programme 1980-81

## BARTON ROVERS F.C.

(Founded 1898)

*Associate Members of F.A.*
*Affiliated to Beds F.A.*

## SPONSORED BY
## WALLSPAN BEDROOMS
### Flitwick (957) 3621

### Price 10p

# BASHLEY F.C.

## BEAZER HOMES LEAGUE - PREMIER DIVISION

## BASHLEY v ASHFORD TOWN

### SATURDAY 19TH OCTOBER 1991 KICK OFF 3.00 p.m.

# Fairfield

◄

Programme from
Biggleswade Town v. Coventry City "A"
2nd January 1954

►

Programme from
Basingstoke Town v. Whyteleafe
11th October 1994

►►

Programme from
Basingstoke Town v. Bromley 14th April 1990
& v. Redbridge Forest 16th April 1990

## The Camrose Ground

# BASINGSTOKE TOWN F.C.

## 1994-95

Main Sponsor

**80p**

Volume 1
Issue 8

**V**
**WHYTELEAFE F.C.**
Diadora League Division One
Tuesday 11th October 1994
K.O. 7.30pm

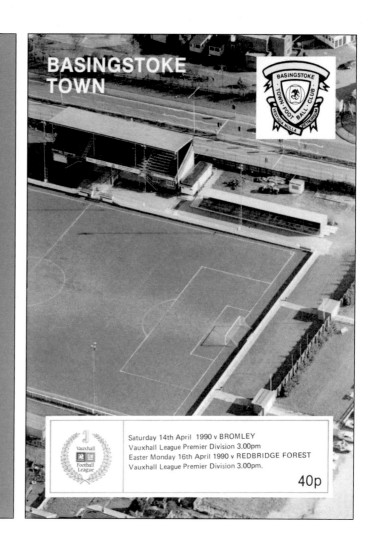

BASINGSTOKE
TOWN

Saturday 14th April 1990 v BROMLEY
Vauxhall League Premier Division 3.00pm
Easter Monday 16th April 1990 v REDBRIDGE FOREST
Vauxhall League Premier Division 3.00pm.

**40p**

◀

Programme from
Bath City v. Barry Town
29th October 1955

▶

Programme from
Bath City v. Nuneaton Borough
20th March 1976

▶▶

Programme from
Bath City v. Welling United
29th January 2013
Match postponed and played on
19th March 2013

# Twerton Park

# BATH CITY FOOTBALL CLUB

| President: | A. J. WAIT |
| Vice-President: | R. WILLIAMS |
| Chairman: | G. WALSHAW |
| Directors: | A. WALSHAW, D. COUNSELL, B. J. HEAD, J. HUGHES, S. WOODMAN. |
| General Manager: | JACK SMITH |
| Medical Officer: | Dr. L. SCOTT-WHITE |

Photo: West Air Photography.

# NUNEATON BOROUGH SOUTHERN LEAGUE

SATURDAY, 20th MARCH 1976
K.O. 3.00 p.m.

**Official Programme 10p**

# BATH CITY FOOTBALL CLUB
OFFICIAL MATCHDAY PROGRAMME 2012-13 SEASON £2.50

Tuesday 29 January 2013 ko 7.45pm
v WELLING UNITED

MOORE STEPHENS   Minuteman Press   FILA @ jd   mayday TRUST

Southern League Premier Division

# Eagles
## v
# Dover

Saturday 27th November 1976 K.O. 3.00pm

# The Eyrie

◄

Programme from
Bedford Town v. Dover
27th November 1976

►

Programme from
Bedford Town v. Worcester City
26th August 1978

►►

Programme from
Bedford Town v. Cambridge City
23rd January 1967

# The Eyrie

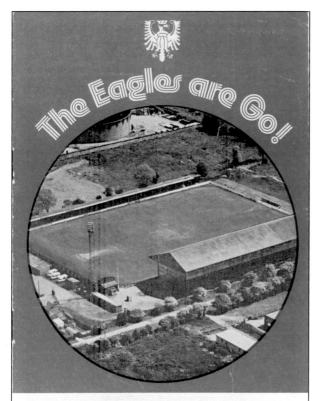

# The Eagles are Go!

## Bedford Town F.C.
### v
## Worcester

Saturday August 26th · Kick-off 3.00pm

# BEDFORD TOWN
# FOOTBALL CLUB

"The Eagles"

Eastern Professional Floodlight Competition

## BEDFORD TOWN
### v.
## CAMBRIDGE CITY

PROGRAMME NUMBER **662**

Monday, 23rd January, 1967. Kick-off 7.30 p.m.

**NEXT HOME MATCHES**

Saturday, January 28th. Kick-off 3 p.m.—
F.A. Challenge Cup (Third Round)—BEDFORD v. PETERBOROUGH.

Saturday, February 4th. Kick-off 3 p.m.
Southern League—BEDFORD v. GUILDFORD CITY.

**Official Programme**      **Price 6d.**

# The Eyrie

BEDFORD TOWN ASSOCIATION FOOTBALL CLUB LTD.

v.

# WEYMOUTH

SATURDAY, 28th AUGUST, 1965    Kick-off 3 p.m.

OFFICIAL PROGRAMME 6d.

◄

Programme from
Bedford Town v. Weymouth
28th August 1965

►►
Programme from
Bedford Town v. King's Lynn
25th September 1965

# The Eyrie

# BEDFORD TOWN
## ASSOCIATION FOOTBALL CLUB LTD.

SATURDAY, 25th SEPTEMBER, 1965
Kick-off 3 p.m.

# KING'S LYNN

OFFICIAL PROGRAMME
PRICE 6d.

Official Match Day Programme No. 13

BEAZER HOMES LEAGUE - Midland Division

**Bedworth United v Dudley Town**

Saturday 22nd January 1994

Kick - off 3.00pm          Programme 50p

****** GREENBACKS SPONSORS FOR 1993 - 94 ******

**DOUBLE VISION**
Unit 1, Hornchurch Close, Coventry  Tel: (0203) 367113

◀

Programme from
Bedworth United v. Dudley Town
22nd January 1994

▶

Programme from
Bedworth United v. Dartford 21st August 1981
and v. Enderby Town 24th August 1981

Programme from
Bedworth United v. Leamington
1st January 2008

# The Oval

# BEDWORTH UNITED
## ASSOCIATION
## FOOTBALL CLUB LTD.

### Members of the Southern League Premier
### Birmingham County F.A.

Photography by John Horsley Photography

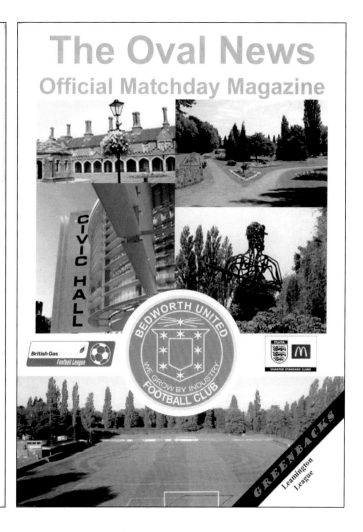

# The Oval News
## Official Matchday Magazine

CIVIC HALL

BEDWORTH UNITED
WE GROW BY INDUSTRY
FOOTBALL CLUB

British Gas
Football League

The FA
CHARTER STANDARD CLUBS

GREENBACKS
Leamington
League

# BILSTON TOWN FC

SEASON 1991-92 MATCH-DAY MAGAZINE 50p

Main Sponsor:
## CARTWRIGHT HOMES

Beazer Homes League

# Queen Street

◄

Programme from
Bilston Town v. Dudley Town
20th April 1992

►

Programme from
Bexley United v. Wisbech
29th August 1964

►►

Programme from
Bexley United v. Nuneaton Borough
24th August 1963

# The Welling Ground

## THE BOROUGH CLUB
# BEXLEY UNITED
## WELLING GROUND

**SEASON 1964-65**                    **No. 2**

### SOUTHERN LEAGUE
Premier Division
v.

## WISBECH
SATURDAY, AUG. 29th
K.O. 3.0

---

*NEXT HOME MATCH*
Next Wednesday          K.O. 6.15
### WIMBLEDON
METROPOLITAN LEAGUE

---

# BEXLEY UNITED
## WELLING GROUND

**SEASON 1963-64**                    **No. I**

### SOUTHERN LEAGUE
Premier Division
v.

## NUNEATON
K.O. 3.0
SATURDAY, AUGUST 24th

Next Home Match
**NEXT TUESDAY**          K.O. 6.30
### DARTFORD
Metropolitan League

# The Sports Ground

Fred Berry, one of Bideford's most loyal players, shows his dominance in the air. (Photo : Chris Hold)

Western League    Sat., Dec. 13, 1980

**WELTON ROVERS**    10P

◀

Programme from
Bideford v. Welton Rovers
13th December 1980

▶

Programme from
Bideford v. Ilminster Town
22nd December 1979

▶▶

Programme from
Bideford v. Westland Yeovil
5th February 1977

# The Sports Ground

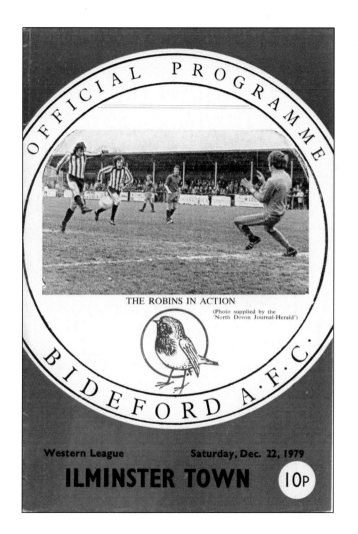

OFFICIAL PROGRAMME

THE ROBINS IN ACTION

(Photo supplied by the
'North Devon Journal-Herald')

BIDEFORD A.F.C.

Western League            Saturday, Dec. 22, 1979

## ILMINSTER TOWN

10P

Reproduced by courtesy of " The North Devon Journal Herald."

ROTHMAN'S WESTERN
LEAGUE

# WESTLAND - YEOVIL

Official Programme : Price 5p

SAT., 5th FEBRUARY, 1977

*Issued by Bideford A.F. Supporters' Club*

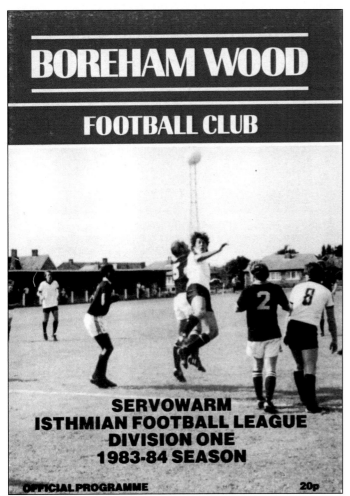

# Broughinge Road

◀

Programme from
Boreham Wood v. Feltham
13th December 1983

▶

Programme from
Bishop Auckland v. Accrington Stanley
18th November 1995

# Kingsway Ground

▶▶

Programme from
Bishop Auckland v. Holker Old Boys
2nd October 2015

# Heritage Park

# BISHOP AUCKLAND
# FOOTBALL CLUB

Founded 1886

## 1995 - 1996

**KINGSWAY GROUND
BISHOP AUCKLAND
CO. DURHAM
DL14 7JN
Tel: (01388) 604403**

Bishops Club Call
0891 664497 updated daily

*THE*
*UniBond*
*LEAGUE*

Accrington Stanley

Saturday 18th
November
1995

# Bishop Auckland Football Club

**Bishop Auckland FC v Holker Old Boys**
Friday 2nd October 2015 7:45pm Kick Off

## MATCH DAY PROGRAMME 2015-2016

www.bishopafc.com
01388 604605

Official team sponsors

**IVEST**
Construction
www.iiveco.biz
01388 778822

**comtek**

www.comtek.uk.com
01388 567120

**£1.00**

Match Day Programme Published 02/10/2015

# Victoria Park

◄

Programme from
Bournemouth v. AFC Totton
6th November 2004

►

Programme from
Boston United v. Bury
19th November 1983

# York Street

►►

Programme from
Boston v. Alfreton Town
6th February 1982

# Tattershall Road

YORK STREET REPORT

THE OFFICIAL MATCHDAY MAGAZINE OF

# BOSTON UNITED

BOSTON UNITED
THE PILGRIMS

F.A. CUP 1ST ROUND PROPER  **UNITED v BURY**  Saturday 19th November 1983 Kick off 3.00 pm  **30p**

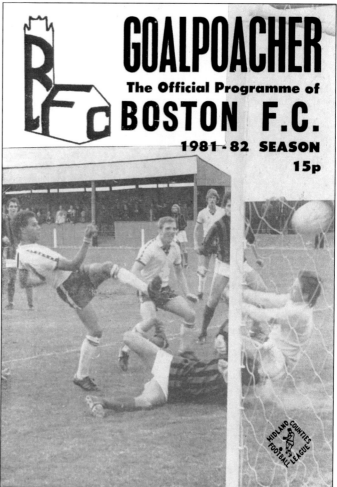

# GOALPOACHER

The Official Programme of

## BOSTON F.C.

1981 - 82 SEASON

15p

BFC

MIDLAND COUNTIES FOOTBALL LEAGUE

SEASON
1999/2000

# BRIDGNORTH TOWN FOOTBALL CLUB

## INTERLINK EXPRESS MIDLAND FOOTBALL ALLIANCE

INTERLINK EXPRESS MIDLAND FOOTBALL ALLIANCE

**Saturday 22nd April 2000**
**Kick - Off 3.00 pm**

60p

v

**Stratford Town F.C.**

# Crown Meadow

◄

Programme from
Bridgnorth Town v. Stratford Town
22nd April 2000

►

Programme from
Braintree Town v. Tonbridge Angels
19th September 1995

►►

Programme from
Braintree Town v. Colchester United
6th August 1990

# Cressing Road

# BRAINTREE
## TOWN F.C.

### Official Match Programme £1

This season`s Main Sponsors are:

**Braintree**
**Yellow Line**
It's you we're always here for.

Beazer
Homes
League

Beazer Homes League-Southern Div.
Tuesday 19th September 1995
Kick Off 7.45pm

## TONBRIDGE ANGELS

---

OFFICIAL MATCHDAY PROGRAMME OF

# BRAINTREE TOWN
## F.C.

### JEWSON FOOTBALL LEAGUE PREMIER DIVISION

## Official Club Sponsors 1990·91
## CHELMSFORD STAR Co-Op

# SEASON 90·91    35P

## Castlefields

**BRIDGWATER TOWN A.F.C. LTD.**

Runners-up Western League Div. 1, 1957-58. Winners Western Lge. Professional Cup, 1957-58. Finalists 1959-60. Winners of Som. Senior League, 1957-58, 1960-61, 1961-62.

Winners of Somerset Senior Lge. KO Cup, 1957-58, 1966-67. Winners of Somerset Professional Cup, 1958-59

OFFICIAL PROGRAMME    PRICE 4d.

**Bridgwater Town v. Glastonbury** Western League
(Western League Champions 1967/68)    Saturday, 16th Nov., 1968    k.o. 3.0 p.m.

For CAMERAS - TOILET PREPARATIONS
WINES and ALL MEDICAL SUPPLIES
**L. H. LLEWELLYN, Limited**
Phone 3055/6    BRIDGWATER

Published by the Bridgwater Town Supporters' Club

# Castlefields

◄

Programme from
Bridgwater Town v. Glastonbury
16th November 1968

►

Programme from
Bromley v. Wokingham Town
5th November 1994

# Hayes Lane

►►

Programme from
Bromsgrove Rovers v. Gosport Borough
31st March 1990

# Victoria Ground

# BROMLEY
## FOOTBALL CLUB

*Official Programme*

The Diadora Football League

*Season 1994-1995*
*Premier Division*

80p

# Bromsgrove
# Rovers

LEAGUE

Official
Matchday
Magazine

BROMSGROVE ROVERS

Main Sponsors

ROVER GROUP MAIN DEALER
CLARK'S

# Eton Park

◄

Programme from
Burton Albion v. Caernarfon Town
19th October 1985

►

Programme from
Burton Albion v. Ashford Town
3rd September 1988

►►

Programme from
Burton Albion v. Dartford
3rd February 1990

# Eton Park

1988 1989

## Beazer Homes League

# BURTON ALBION

OFFICIAL SPONSORS
18 56
BURTON BREWERY LTD

BEAZER HOMES LEAGUE PREMIER DIVISION
TODAYS VISITORS ARE
**ASHFORD TOWN**
SATURDAY, 3rd SEPTEMBER '88
Kick-Off 3.00 p.m.
TODAYS MATCHBALL SPONSORS
**GILSON COLOUR PROCESSING**

## PRICE 50p

OFFICIAL SPONSORS

89
90
Beazer Homes League

# BURTON ALBION
## FOOTBALL CLUB

BEAZER HOMES LEAGUE - PREMIER DIVISION

TODAY'S VISITORS ARE

# DARTFORD

SATURDAY FEBRUARY 3rd, 1990.
KICK-OFF 3.00 p.m.
TODAY'S MATCH SPONSORS ARE:
BURTON MAIL GROUP

## PRICE 50p

# Ford Meadow

◄

Programme from
Buckingham Town v. Baldock Town
22nd November 1983

►

Programme from
Bury Town v. Baldock Town
28th December 1987

►►

Programme from
Bury Town v. Potters Bar Town
12th February 2008

# Ram Meadow

# BURY TOWN FC

Beazer Homes League

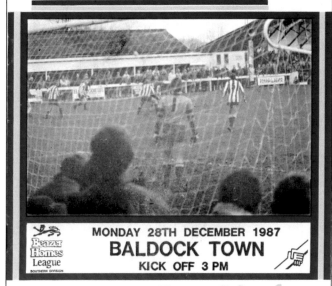

MONDAY 28TH DECEMBER 1987

## BALDOCK TOWN

KICK OFF 3 PM

Beazer Homes League
SOUTHERN DIVISION

## Welcome to Ram Meadow

TEAM SPONSORS

PROGRAMME **25p**

KENNING TYRE SERVICES

Ryman football league

# BURY TOWN FOOTBALL CLUB

RAM MEADOW BURY ST EDMUNDS

## Potters Bar Town

Tuesday 12th February 2008
Ryman League Division 1 North
Kick Off 7.45pm

Associate member of the Football Association and members of the Isthmian Football League

£1.20

MAIN SPONSOR: GTC G TAYLOR CONSTRUCTION LTD

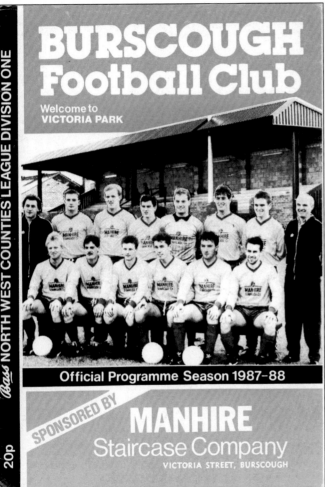

# Victoria Park

◄

Programme from
Burscough v. Atherton LR
9th January 1988

►

Programme from
Buxton v. Runcorn
14th September 1974

►►

Programme from
Buxton v. Goole Town
8th November 1988

# Silverlands

**OFFICIAL PROGRAMME 5p.**

Saturday, 14th September 1974

# BUXTON

v

# RUNCORN

F. A. CHALLENGE CUP
1st Qualifying Round
Kick - off 3.00 p.m.
Programme No. 4.

# SILVERLANDS

# SOCCER

# Buxton
# AFC

*SEASON 1988/89*

OFFICIAL PROGRAMME      30p

# Kingsmead Stadium

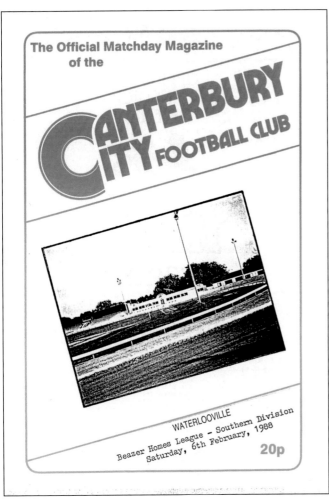

◄

Programme from
Canterbury City v. Waterlooville
6th February 1988

Programme from
Cambridge City v. Yeovil Town
5th April 1966

►►

Programme from
Cambridge City Reserves v. Eynesbury Rovers
14th October 1961

# Milton Road

# CAMBRIDGE CITY
# FOOTBALL CLUB
### *Southern League Champions 1962-63*

# OFFICIAL PROGRAMME 6ᴰ

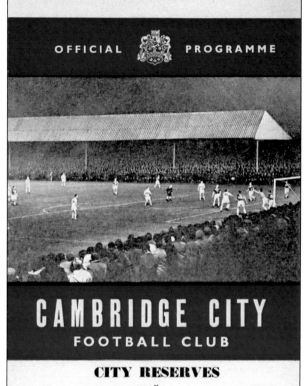

OFFICIAL PROGRAMME

# CAMBRIDGE CITY
## FOOTBALL CLUB

### CITY RESERVES
v.
### EYNESBURY ROVERS

(EASTERN COUNTIES LEAGUE)

SATURDAY, 14th OCTOBER, 1961          Kick-off 3.0 p.m.

### PRICE THREEPENCE

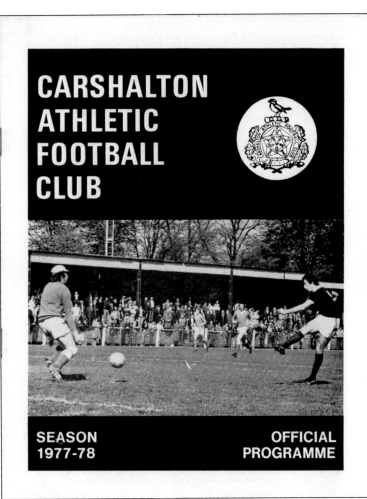

# War Memorial Sports Ground

Programme from
Carshalton Athletic v. Dartford
10th August 1977

▶

Programme from
Chasetown v. Oldbury United
13th December 1997

# The Scholars Ground

▶▶

Programme from
Chelmsford City v. Margate
9th October 1965

# New Writtle Street

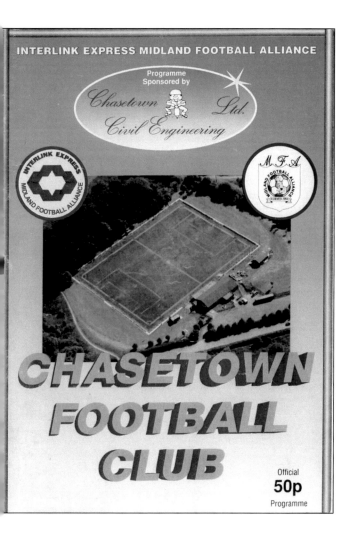

# CHELMSFORD CITY FOOTBALL NEWS № 305

### OFFICIAL PROGRAMME 6d.

Chelmsford & Essex Weekly News Picture

**C**HELMSFORD
**C**ITY FOOTBALL CLUB

SEASON 1974-75

Official Magazine Programme

Price Five Pence

◄

Programme from
Chelmsford City v. Wealdstone
7th October 1974

►

Programme from
Chelmsford City v. Gravesend & Northfleet
2nd January 1989

# New Writtle Street

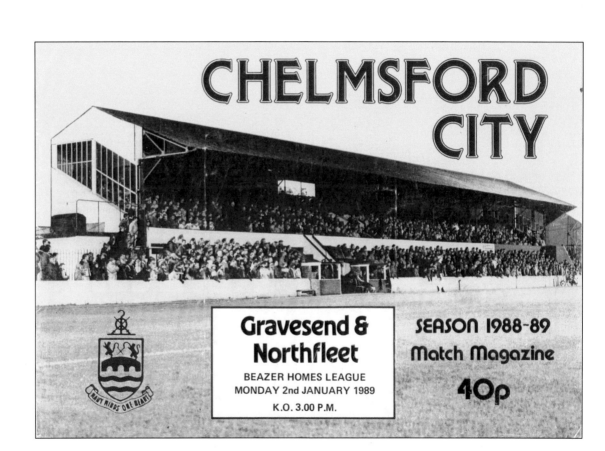

# CHELMSFORD CITY

**Gravesend & Northfleet**

BEAZER HOMES LEAGUE
MONDAY 2nd JANUARY 1989
K.O. 3.00 P.M.

SEASON 1988-89

Match Magazine

40p

# The Meadow

**CHESHAM UNITED**
FOOTBALL CLUB
FOUNDED 1919

MEMBERS OF THE FOOTBALL ASSOCIATION
BERKS & BUCKS F.A. — ATHENIAN LEAGUE
PREMIER FLOODLIGHT LEAGUE

## OFFICIAL PROGRAMME

PRICE 6d.          SEASON 1966/67

LUCKY Nº 364

10/- voucher will be issued to Lucky No. winner.
The voucher must be spent with an advertiser in the programme.

◄
Programme from
Chesham United v. Croydon Amateurs
19th November 1966

►
Programme from
Chertsey Town v. North Greenford United
27th March 2007

►►
Programme from
Chertsey Town v. Bognor Regis Town
4th March 2003

# Alwyns Lane

CHERTSEY TOWN
Football Club

Season 2006/07
Programme £1.00

EL Records Premier Challenge Cup
Semi Final
NORTH GREENFORD Utd
Tuesday 27th March 2007
Kick Off 7.45pm

COLIN
WHITE
GROUP

# Chertsey Town

Tuesday 4th March 2003
Ryman League
Division One South

CHERTSEY TOWN
versus
BOGNOR REGIS TOWN
Kick Off 7.45pm

Sponsored by
The HOLLY TREE
& Chertsey Tool Hire Ltd

Official Programme          £1

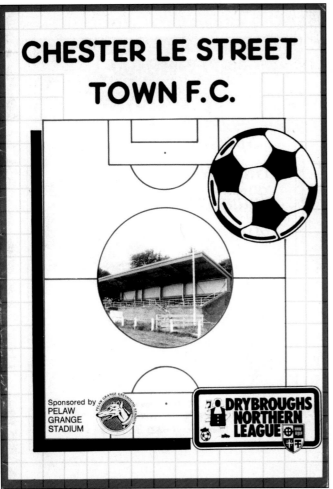

# Moor Park

◄

Programme from
Chester Le Street Town v. South Bank
19th October 1985

►

Programme from
Chippenham Town v. Gloucester City
4th October 2000

# Hardenhuish Park

►►

Programme from
Chipstead v. Ramsgate
1st October 2013

# High Road

# *Chippenham Town*

**SCREWFIX** *DIRECT*

**STENTORFIELD**
CRANE
Official Club Sponsor

Official Programme

Les Phillips Cup Winners & F.A. Carlsberg Vase Finalists 2000

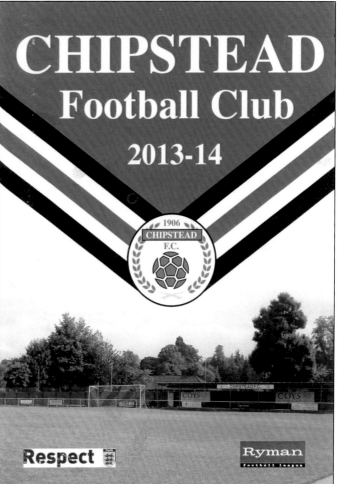

# CHIPSTEAD
## Football Club
### 2013-14

1906
CHIPSTEAD
F.C.

**Respect**

**Ryman**
football league

Clipstone Welfare F.C

The Lido Ground, Clipstone

Matchday Programme - Season 2011/12

WINDSOR FOOD SERVICE
CENTRAL MIDLANDS FOOTBALL LEAGUE

GLENWOOD PRINTING RESERVE
SUPREME DIVISION 2011/12

Clipstone Welfare Reserves

V

Mickleover Sports Reserves

Saturday 3rd December 2011 - 3pm K.O          £1

◄

Programme from
Clipstone Welfare Reserves v.
Mickleover Sports Reserves
3rd December 2011

►

Programme from
Chorley v. Ashton United
16th March 1982

►►

Programme from
Chorley v. Stalybridge Celtic
10th September 1962

# Victory Park

# MAGPIE REVIEW

## 1981-82

# CHORLEY F.C.

---

3d.                                   No.   218

## OFFICIAL PROGRAMME
# Chorley Football Club
### VICTORY PARK
Members of the Lancashire Combination, Divisions One and Two

## CHORLEY versus STALYBRIDGE CELTIC
### INTER-LEAGUE CUP FIRST ROUND (REPLAY)
### SEPTEMBER 10th, 1962

### HONOURS

Championship Winners:—1920, 1923, 1928, 1929, 1933, 1934, 1940, 1946, 1960, 1961.

Runners-up:—1922, 1927, 1949.

Junior Cup Winners:—1894, 1909, 1924, 1940, 1946, 1958, 1959, 1961.

Runners-up:—1921, 1922, 1926, 1934, 1942, 1943, 1945, 1960.

Inter-League Cup:—Runners-up 1962.

Chairman: Mr. H. D. Wrennall
Secretary: Mr. J. Mosscrop, 283 Eaves Lane, Chorley
Treasurer: Mr. D. Sanderson

Chorley Guardian Co., Ltd.

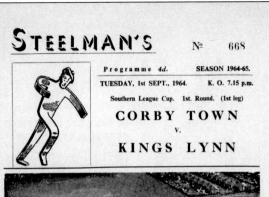

STEELMAN'S N⁰ 668

Programme 4d.   SEASON 1964-65.

TUESDAY, 1st SEPT., 1964.   K. O. 7.15 p.m.

Southern League Cup.   1st. Round.   (1st leg)

**CORBY TOWN**

v.

**KINGS LYNN**

THE POPULAR "Pink 'Un" THE

SPORTS TELEGRAPH

Still as popular as ever.   **3d.**—Every Saturday Evening—**3d.**

All Your National and Local Sports reports.

# Occupation Road

◄

Programme from
Corby Town v. King's Lynn
1st September 1964

►

Programme from
Crediton United v. Alphington
16th August 2013

# Lords Meadow Sports Centre

►►

Programme from
Croydon v. Millwall
15th December 1979

# Croydon Sports Arena

# CREDITON UNITED

SOUTH WEST PENINSULAR LEAGUE - DIVISION ONE - EAST

## CREDITON UNITED v ALPHINGTON

FRIDAY 16th AUGUST 2013 - KO 7:30pm

# CROYDON FOOTBALL CLUB

Associate Members Football Association
Members Surrey F.A.
Members London F.A.

General Hon. Secretary
R. E. Guest,
11, Ridgemount Avenue,
Shirley, Croydon, Surrey.
Telephone: 01-656-9230

CROYDON SPORTS ARENA, ALBERT ROAD,
SOUTH NORWOOD, S.E.25.
Telephone: 01-654 5524 Dressing,
01-654 8555 Clubhouse.

BERGER ISTHMIAN LEAGUE

1979/80 SEASON

OFFICIAL PROGRAMME 20p.

LUCKY NUMBER . . . . . . (See Page 8)

# Crockenhill F.C.

**British Energy**

~ 9th August 2001 ~ Friendly fixture ~

Crockenhill versus

## St. Leonards

50p
or free with
Admission

# Wested Meadow

◄

Programme from
Crockenhill v. St. Leonards
9th August 2001

►

Programme from
Crockenhill v. Tunbridge Wells
22nd October 1998

# Park View &
# Wested Meadow

►►

Programme from
Crockenhill v. FC Elmstead
12th December 2015

# Wested Meadow

# Crockenhill F.C.

FORMED 1946

AFFILIATED TO THE K.C.F.A.

MEMBERS OF THE WINSTONLEAD KENT FOOTBALL LEAGUE SINCE 1968

KENT PREMIER LEAGUE

Thursday 22nd October 1998

## Crockenhill

*Versus*

## Tunbridge Wells

kick-off 7:45 pm

---

# Crockenhill F.C.

Formed 1946
Affiliated to the K.C.F.A.

Official Sponsors
LAPA Security Solutions
Gables Pet Parlour
Carroll Carpets
Europa Sports
Hughes Development
Gladwish Land Sales
Pain & Glory Sports
Durkan

CHARTER STANDARD CLUBS

*Home of the Crocks*

## Welcome To Wested Meadow

Saturday 12th December 2015 ~ Kick Off: 2pm
Kent Invicta League

## Crockenhill F.C

~ Versus ~

## FC Elmstead

Kent Invicta Football League

*'Kent's missing link has been found'*

Affiliated to The Football Association

Please Follow us on our website at www.Crockenhillfc.co.uk
OFFICIAL MATCH DAY PROGRAMME   £2.00

## DARTFORD

v

## BURTON ALBION

BEAZER HOMES LEAGUE, PREMIER DIVISION

SATURDAY 21st SEPTEMBER 1991 K. O. 3.00p.m.

DARTFORD F. C.

1991 OFFICIAL MATCH 80P

1992 PROGRAMME

◄

Programme from
Dartford v. Burton Albion
21st September 1991

►

Programme from
Dagenham & Redbridge v. Stalybridge Celtic
5th December 1992

►►

Programme from
Dagenham v. Leatherhead
25th April 1975

# Victoria Road

# Dagenham & Redbridge

## FOOTBALL CLUB

OFFICIAL MATCH DAY MAGAZINE

### SEASON 1992 - 1993

**DAGENHAM & REDBRIDGE FOOTBALL CLUB
are sponsored by THE DAGENHAM POST
and today welcome our visitors**

**v. STALYBRIDGE CELTIC**
GM VAUXHALL CONFERENCE
Saturday 5th. December 1992
Vol. 1 No. 12

Official Match Day Magazine £1

GM VAUXHALL
CONFERENCE

# DAGENHAM F.C.

*OFFICIAL PROGRAMME — Price 5p*

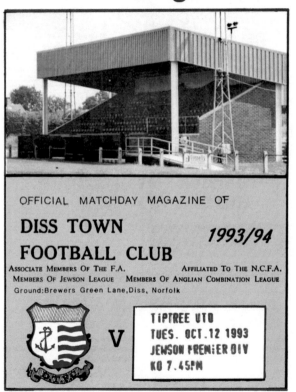

◄

Programme from
Diss Town v. Tiptree United
12th October 1993

►

Programme from
Denaby United v. Belper Town
27th January 1996

►►

Programme from
Denaby United v. Emley
14th August 1991

# Tickhill Square

DENABY UNITED F C

Ben Bailey
Homes

**1895/6 Centenary Season 1995/6 Match Programme**

Saturday 27th January
v BELPER TOWN
NCEL:
Prem Div.
50P

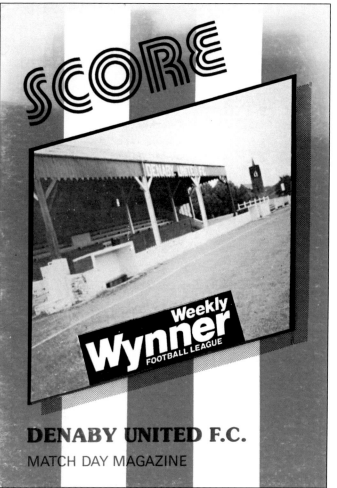

SCORE

weekly
**Wynner**
FOOTBALL LEAGUE

## DENABY UNITED F.C.

MATCH DAY MAGAZINE

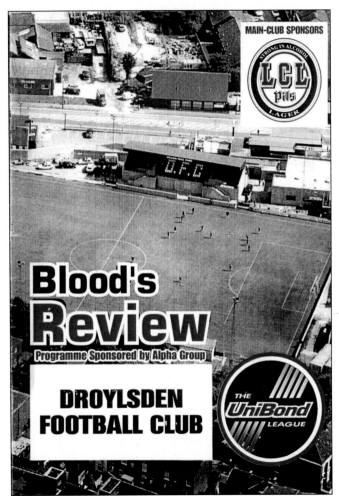

# Butchers Arms Ground

◄

Programme from
Droylsden v. Colwyn Bay
21st August 2001

►

Programme from
Dudley Town v. Milton Keynes City
13th November 1982

# Sports Centre

►►

Programme from
Dulwich Hamlet v. Walthamstow Avenue
11th April 1985

# Champion Hill

## Official Programme-Season 1982-83

**15p**

# DULWICH HAMLET

### FOOTBALL        CLUB

SEASON 1984-85
MEMBERS OF SERVOWARM ISTHMIAN LEAGUE
PREMIER DIVISION

25p

◄

Programme from
Eastbourne United v. Basildon United
29th August 1981

►

Programme from
Eastbourne United v. Newbury Town
25th April 1959

►►

Programme from
Eastbourne United v. Turners Hill
4th November 1972

# The Oval

LUCKY PROGRAMME NO.     PRICE 3d.

Ground—THE OVAL, PRINCES PARK  Phone 6989
*President*: Alderman L. W. PYLE
*Chairman*: Councillor P. G. WOOD
*Hon. Secretary*: W. J. CROSSMAN, Kenton, Station Road, Polegate
*Manager*: JACK MANSELL

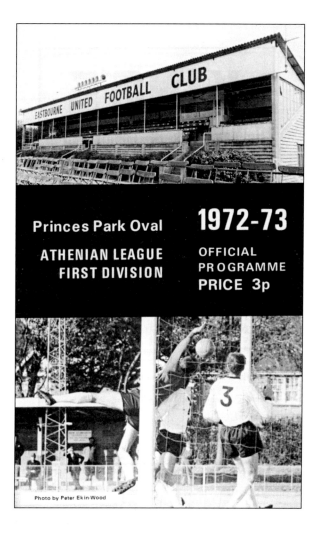

Princes Park Oval

ATHENIAN LEAGUE
FIRST DIVISION

1972-73

OFFICIAL
PROGRAMME
PRICE 3p

Photo by Peter Ekin-Wood

ENFIELD FOOTBALL CLUB LTD

OFFICIAL PROGRAMME

MEMBERS ISTHMIAN LEAGUE – PREMIER DIVISION

ISTHMIAN LEAGUE CHAMPIONS
Seasons 1967/68 1968/69 1969/70 1975/76 1976/77 1977/78 1979/80

◄

Programme from
Enfield v. Bromley
7th February 1981

►

Programme from
Egham Town v. Maidenhead United
22nd April 1989

# Tempest Road

►►

Programme from
Ely City v. Histon
23rd November 1957

# Paradise Ground

# EGHAM TOWN
# FOOTBALL CLUB

VAUXHALL-OPEL

**VAUXHALL  GM  OPEL**

*League*

TODAY'S OPPONENTS ARE:

Maidenhead United

Kick-off 3.00pm

# ELY CITY FOOTBALL CLUB

FORMED IN THE YEAR 1885

**RUNNERS-UP PETERBOROUGH LEAGUE 1956-57**

ASSOCIATE MEMBER FOOTBALL ASSOCIATION

*Member of*

CAMBRIDGESHIRE FOOTBALL ASSOCIATION
PETERBOROUGH AND DISTRICT LEAGUE
*(Premier Division and Division 1)*
CAMBS. LEAGUE DIVISION IV SECTION B

Hon. Secretary:

W. C. LAWRENCE
Cemetery Lodge, Ely
Phone: ELY 2339

**OFFICIAL
PROGRAMME**

№ 3339

Reproduced by kind permission of
"ELY STANDARD."

George King scores our first goal
against March Town United—
2nd November, 1957
(Photo by John Slater)

**EPPING TOWN**
**FOOTBALL CLUB LTD**

MAIN SPONSORS — COMET ROOFING (LONDON) LTD

**SEASON 1983 – 4**

**OFFICIAL PROGRAMME**

20p

◄

Programme from
Epping Town v. Grays Athletic
7th January 1984

►

Programme from
A.F.C. Emley v. Hallam
5th September 2007

►►

Programme from
Emley AFC v. Thackley
9th September 1995

# Welfare Ground

## A.F.C. EMLEY

£1.00

The FA CUP e·on

Vs

### Hallam F.C.

Wednesday 5th September 2007
The F.A.Cup (sponsored by E-ON)
Preliminary Round Replay
Kick Off 19.45

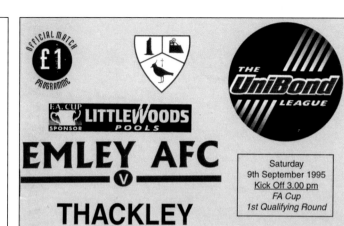

OFFICIAL MATCH
£1
PROGRAMME

THE UniBond LEAGUE

F.A. CUP SPONSOR **LITTLEWOODS** POOLS

## EMLEY AFC
V
## THACKLEY

Saturday
9th September 1995
Kick Off 3.00 pm
FA Cup
1st Qualifying Round

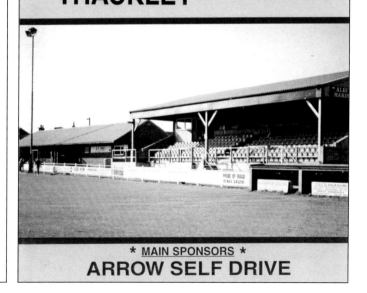

# West Street

◀

Programme from
Epsom & Ewell v. Harrow Borough
30th December 1967

▶

Programme from
Erith & Belvedere v. Hounslow
16th February 1988

# Park View

▶▶

Programme from
Farsley Celtic v. Warrington Town
4th September 1993

# Throstle Nest

# ERITH & BELVEDERE F.C. LTD

OFFICIAL
PROGRAMME
16 FEB 1988
Telephone: 01-311 4444

Founded 1922

"PARK VIEW" LOWER ROAD. BELVEDERE. KENT. DA17 6DF.

Affiliated : F.A., KENT F.A., LONDON F.A.

Members BEAZER HOMES LEAGUE ESSEX & HERTS COMB,
KENT YOUTH LEAGUE.

*Football Secretary:* Mr. L.G. Meakins.
23 Windermere Close,
DARTFORD,
Kent DA1 2TX.

Telephone: Dartford 29406.

**WARNING**

The Directors of Erith & Belvedere F.C. Ltd. accept no liability for any accidents to spectators on the Football Ground and/or its precincts.

The Floodlighting Towers are dangerous due to the high voltage used and also accidents can be caused by climbing them.

Cars are parked at owners risk.

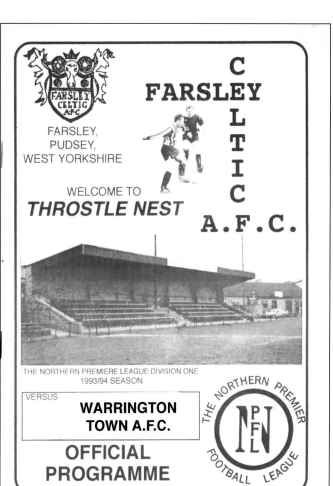

FARSLEY,
PUDSEY,
WEST YORKSHIRE

# FARSLEY CELTIC A.F.C.

WELCOME TO
*THROSTLE NEST*

THE NORTHERN PREMIERE LEAGUE DIVISION ONE
1993/94 SEASON

VERSUS

**WARRINGTON
TOWN A.F.C.**

## OFFICIAL PROGRAMME

THE NORTHERN PREMIER FOOTBALL LEAGUE
NPFL

# The Town Ground

◄

Programme from
Felixstowe Town v. Tring Town
2nd September 1989

►

Programme from
Fisher Athletic v. Telford United
22nd April 1989

►►

Programme from
Fisher Athletic v. Newport AFC
4th October 1997

# Surrey Docks Stadium

**FISHER ATHLETIC**

VAUXHALL CONFERENCE

**OFFICIAL MATCHDAY PROGRAMME**
**TELFORD UNITED F.C.**
SATURDAY 22ND APRIL 1989
KICK OFF 3.00 p.m.

**50p**

**SEASON 1988/89**

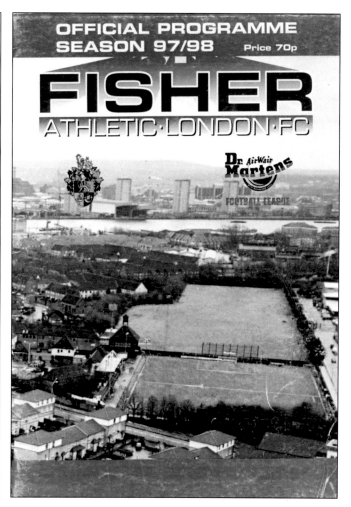

**OFFICIAL PROGRAMME**
**SEASON 97/98**   Price 70p

# FISHER
## ATHLETIC · LONDON · FC

**Dr. AirWair Martens**
FOOTBALL LEAGUE

**FOLKESTONE TOWN**
**FOOTBALL CLUB**

Headquarters : CHERITON ROAD, FOLKESTONE

'Phone : FOLKESTONE 51374.          Colours : AMBER AND BLACK.

Members of the F.A., Kent League Divisions I and II.

**Official Programme**                    **Price 2d.**

MONDAY, DECEMBER 26th, 1949        Kick-off 2.30 p.m.

**FOLKESTONE TOWN**

v.

**ASHFORD**

KENT LEAGUE—Division I

Officials :

President : MAJOR C. TUFF, D.L., J.P.
Chairman : R. MUDDLE, Esq.
Vice-Chairman : H. HENLEY, Esq.

Hon. Secretary : MISS D. PARKER, Broadmead, Cherry Garden Ave.   Phone : 85515
Hon. Surgeon : A. F. DUNN, M.B., Ch.B.
Hon. Masseur : J. W. H. PEMBLE, M.S.F.
Committee : F. BLUNT, F. CHILVERS, R. COURT, W. HEATH, A. C. AIRD, H. HENLEY,
J. STRICKLAND, W. H. EATON, W. ARMORY.
Manager : W. ARMORY, 29a, Manor Road. 'Phone : 2158.   Treasurer : L. J. PENNY
Hon. Press Secretary : F. R. BLUNT, 109 Dolphins Road, Folkestone.
Season Tickets : W. HEATH, 51, Cherry Garden Lane, Folkestone. Phone : 85253

NEXT HOME GAME—

Saturday, December 31st, 1949                    Kick-off 2.30 p.m.

**FOLKESTONE TOWN RES. v. WHITSTABLE**

Kent League—Div. II

# Cheriton Road

◄

Programme from
Folkestone Town v. Ashford
26th December 1949

▶

Programme from
Ford United v. Hullbridge Sports
28th March 1992

# Rush Green

▶▶

Programme from
Forest Green Rovers v. Bristol Rovers
October 1983
No precise date was included in the programme

# The Lawn

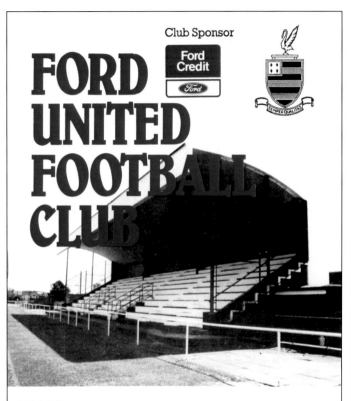

## Club Sponsor

**Ford Credit**
*Ford*

# FORD UNITED FOOTBALL CLUB

Official Programme

Visitors

Competition

28th MARCH 1992

HULLBRIDGE SPORTS

LEAGUE

SOUTHERN LEAGUE MIDLAND DIVISION

# GREENLINER

OFFICIAL MATCHDAY MAGAZINE OF FOREST GREEN ROVERS FC

**25p**

WELCOME
TO WESTFIELD LANE

MEMBERS of the NORTHERN PREMIER FOOTBALL LEAGUE ·

Frickley Athletic F.C.

Season 1987 / 88

30p    Founded 1910

# Westfield Lane

◄

Programme from
Frickley Athletic v. Morecambe
18th February 1988

►

Programme from
Formby v. All Stars XI
4th August 2002

# Brows Lane

IN MEMORY OF
BROWS LANE 1920 TO 2002

THE NORTH WEST COUNTIES LEAGUE DIVISION TWO
FORMBY A.F.C.  V  ALL STARS X1
SUNDAY 4TH AUGUST 2002 KICK OFF 1PM (FINAL GAME)

# Bailrigg

◄

Programme from
Furness College v. Power Station
25th April 1986

►

Programme from
Gainsborough Trinity v. Marine
12th September 1998

# Northolme

►►

Programme from
Garforth Town v. Parkgate
5th April 2007

# Wheatley Park

# GAINSBOROUGH TRINITY

## Season 1998 / 99

## THE BLUES

*125th Anniversary*

Today's
Match Sponsor

**HENRY KEMP**
ROAD MAINTENANCE

UniBond Premier
League
v
**MARINE**
FC

Official Matchday Programme: Price £1

the *fleet* Matchday Magazine 1992–93

**BEAZER HOMES LEAGUE**
Southern Division

# Stonebridge Road

◀

Programme from
Gravesend & Northfleet v. Ashford Town
20th October 1992

Programme from
Gateshead v. Frickley Athletic
10th November 1979

▶▶

Programme from
Gateshead v. Oswestry Town
22nd August 1981

# Gateshead Stadium

**1979~1980**

**WELCOME TO**

# GATESHEAD

**Football Club**

OFFICIAL PROGRAMME 15p

**F.A. TROPHY—2nd Qualifying Round**
Saturday, 10th November, 1979
Kick-off 3·00 p.m.
**Gateshead v. Frickley Ath.**

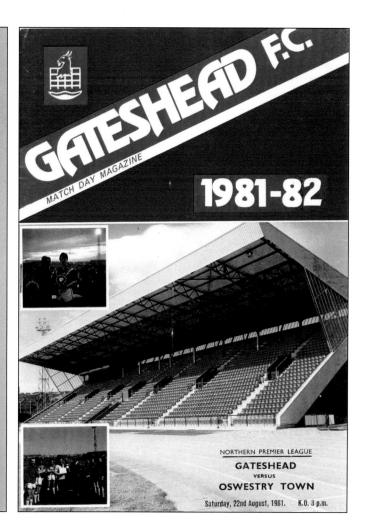

**GATESHEAD F.C.**

MATCH DAY MAGAZINE

**1981-82**

NORTHERN PREMIER LEAGUE
**GATESHEAD**
VERSUS
**OSWESTRY TOWN**
Saturday, 22nd August, 1981.   K.O. 3 p.m.

# The Moat Ground

◄

Programme from
Gresley Rovers v. Stourbridge
30th January 1993

►

Programme from
Grays Athletic v. Barnet
1st November 1958

►►

Programme from
Grays Athletic v. Bromley
5th April 1986

# Recreation Ground

# GRAYS ATHLETIC FOOTBALL CLUB

**Associate Members of the Football Association**

Affiliated to the Essex F.A.        Members Athenian League and Thurrock Combination

## RECREATION GROUND, GRAYS

Tel.: Grays Thurrock 3424

### ATHENIAN LEAGUE

## GRAYS ATH. v. BARNET

### Saturday, November 1st, 1958, kick-off 2.45 p.m.

**OFFICIAL PROGRAMME  -  -  3d.**

# GRAYS ATHLETIC FOOTBALL CLUB 1890

Full members of the Football Association.
Affiliated to the Essex County Football Association.
Members of the Vauxhall-Opel League and
Essex and Herts Border Combination.

Headquarters: The Recreation Ground, Bridge Road, Grays, Essex RM17 6BZ
Telephone: Grays Thurrock 77753

# VAUXHALL-OPEL

*League*

## Match Day Magazine of "THE BLUES"

**The Brettsiders**

*Official Match Day Programme*

**www.hadleigh-utd.co.uk**

**Thurlow Nunn Premier Division**

**Hadleigh United**

versus

**Stanway Rovers**

**Saturday 1st December 2012**

Today's Match Day Sponsor:
**Greene King**

Today's Match BallSponsor:
**Scrutton Bland**

**Hadleigh Tyre Group**

◄

Programme from
Hadleigh United v. Stanway Rovers
1st December 2012

►

Programme from
Halesowen Town v. Wivenhoe Town
31st October 1989

►►

Programme from
Halesowen Town v. Cambridge City
29th December 1990

# Grove Recreation Ground

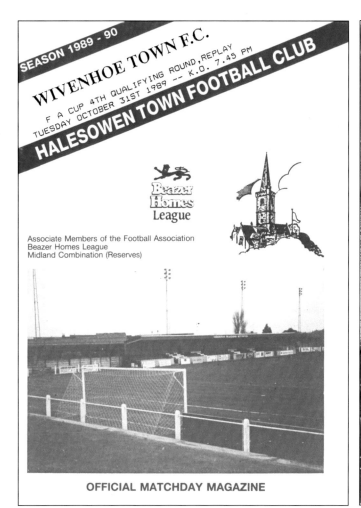

# WIVENHOE TOWN F.C.

F A CUP 4TH QUALIFYING ROUND, REPLAY
TUESDAY OCTOBER 31ST 1989 -- K.O. 7.45 PM

## HALESOWEN TOWN FOOTBALL CLUB

Associate Members of the Football Association
Beazer Homes League
Midland Combination (Reserves)

**OFFICIAL MATCHDAY MAGAZINE**

Associate Members of the Football Association
Beazer Homes League   Midland Combination (Reserves)   Bank's Brewery Mid-week Youth League

# HALESOWEN TOWN F.C.

Wednesday 26th December 1990
v
BROMSGROVE ROVERS
*Season 1990-91*

Saturday 29th December 1990
v
CAMBRIDGE CITY

## PREMIER DIVISION

OFFICIAL PROGRAMME
**50p**

# The Shay

◀

Programme from
Halifax Town v. Burton Albion
16th August 2005

▶

Programme from
Harrogate Town v. Workington
28th August 1999

# Wetherby Road

# TOWN REVIEW

## The Official Programme of HARROGATE TOWN AFC

THE UniBond LEAGUE

CRYSTAL FORD HARROGATE

Main Sponsors to Harrogate Town AFC

# Beveree

◄

Programme from
Hampton v. Marlow
16th April 1988

►

Programme from
Hastings United v. Tonbridge
21st February 1959

# The Pilot Field

►►

Programme from
Hayes v. Redhill
16th September 1933

# Church Road

## HASTINGS UNITED FOOTBALL CLUB LTD

# TONBRIDGE

### SOUTHERN LEAGUE

**Saturday, February 21st, 1959 · KO 3.0 pm**

---

**NEXT HOME MATCH :-**
Saturday, February 28th, 1959        KO 3.0 pm

## CRAWLEY

**3rd Round Metropolitan League Challenge Cup**

---

*Official Programme Price Threepence*    644

---

# HAYES FOOTBALL CLUB

*(Formerly Botwell Mission F.C., Founded 1909.)*
Associate Members Football Association.   Affiliated to Middlesex County F.A.
FINALISTS—AMATEUR CUP 1931.
HOLDERS—LONDON SENIOR CUP 1932.

---

## SEASON 1933-34.

---

## OFFICIAL PROGRAMME.

H. F. C. GROUND.

*Patron:* LORD WAKEFIELD OF HYTHE.
*President and Chairman:* J. BROWN, Esq.
*Vice Chairman:* A. H. WHITE, Esq.
*Hon. Gen. Secretary:* W. H. HOLMES, Esq.,
39, Blyth Road, Hayes, Middlesex.
*Asst. Hon. Secretary:* J. OGDEN, 237, Blyth Road, Hayes, Middlesex.
*Hon. Treasurer:* D. T. ROBERTS, 29, Blyth Road, Hayes, Middlesex.
*Hon. Medical Officer:* DR. J. L. K. LAWSON.
*Ground:* Station Road, Hayes, Middlesex.  'Phone : 582 Hayes.
*Club Headquarters:* Royal Oak Hotel, Station Road, Hayes.  'Phone : Hayes 310.

# HEREFORD UNITED PROGRAMME

SOUTHERN LEAGUE DIVISION I                SATURDAY, 28TH NOVEMBER

### HEREFORD UNITED v.
## DOVER
KICK-OFF 3 p.m.

*DIRECTORS & OFFICIALS*

MR. L. WESTON (*Chairman*)            MR. F. J. SPIERS (*Vice-Chairman*)
MR. T. W. GRIMMER, J.P.      MR. LL. GEORGE       FLT.-LT. R. E. INNS
GROUP-CAPT. A. W. CASWELL, C.B.E., A.F.R.AE.S., M.INST. B.E.
MR. W. J. HUMPHRIES       MR. K. R. V. MICHELL     MR. R. G. PROBERT
MR. C. G. MANNING
*Secretary and Treasurer:* MR. F. J. TURNER
*Manager:* MR. BOB DENNISON
*Hon. Medical Adviser:* MR. P. DEVLIN
*Hon. Club Physiotherapist:* MR. R. BEALES, M.C.S.P.
*Headquarters:* EDGAR STREET ATHLETIC GROUND (*Telephone No.* 4037)

OFFICIAL PROGRAMME

6ᴰ

PUBLISHED BY THE HEREFORD UNITED SUPPORTERS CLUB

---

# Edgar Street

◄

Programme from
Hereford United v. Dover
28th November 1964

►

Programme from
Herne Bay v. Hythe Town
7th November 2007

# Winch's Field

►►

Programme from
Hoddesdon Town v. Harpenden Town
18th March 2000

# Lowfield

# Herne Bay Football Club

Members of the Kent Football League

OFFICIAL PROGRAMME £1.00

KENT LEAGUE
PREMIER DIVISION

HERNE BAY
V
HYTHE TOWN
7TH NOVEMBER 2007
KO 7.45 PM

---

# HODDESDON TOWN F.C.

### FOUNDED 1879

## MEMBERS OF THE MINERVA FOOTBALLS
## SPARTAN SOUTH MIDLANDS FOOTBALL LEAGUE

## v HARPENDEN TOWN F.C.
### SSMFL. Premier Division
### Saturday 18th March 2000.   K.O. 3.00 p.m.

# 1999 / 2000 OFFICIAL
# MATCHDAY PROGRAMME

*Wirral Programme Club Non-League Programme of the Year for 1994/95*
*Team Talk Magazine Programme of the Year for 1996/97*

£1

# Leas Stadium

◀

Programme from
Hillingdon Borough v. Chatham Town
23rd April 1985

Programme from
Hillingdon Borough v. Gloucester City
29th November 1969

▶▶

Programme from
Hillingdon Borough v. Crawley Town
25th April 1970

# Leas Stadium

## SOUTHERN LEAGUE

# Hillingdon Boro.

## V.

# GLOUCESTER CITY

Kick-off 3 p.m.    Saturday, November 29th, 1969

LUCKY PROGRAMME    Photograph kindly supplied by The Uxbridge Post

### OFFICIAL PROGRAMME 9d.

No. 15

Nº  176

# Next Home Game

### F.A. CUP 2nd ROUND

## V.

# LUTON TOWN

Saturday, 6th December, 1969    Kick-off 3 p.m.

---

## SOUTHERN LEAGUE

Saturday, 25th April, 1970.    Kick-off 3.00 p.m.

# HILLINGDON BORO

Photograph kindly supplied by the Uxbridge Weekly Post

# CRAWLEY TOWN

### OFFICIAL PROGRAMME 9d.

No. 37

# Grundy Hill

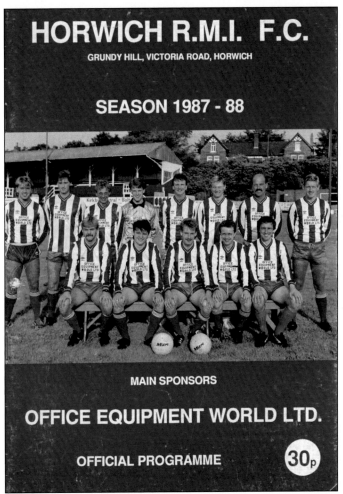

◀

Programme from
Horwich R.M.I. v. Mossley
28th November 1987

▶

Programme from
Hythe Town v. Tooting & Mitcham United
13th October 2015

▶▶

Programme from
Hythe Town v. Maidstone United
29th July 2015

# Reachfields

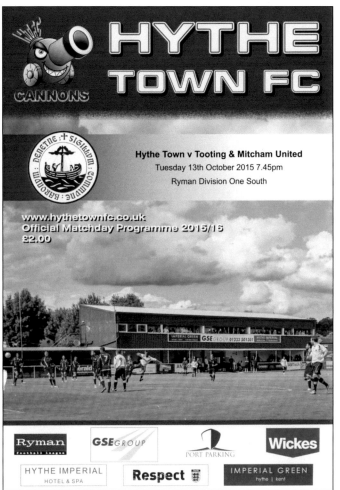

**Hythe Town v Tooting & Mitcham United**

Tuesday 13th October 2015 7.45pm

Ryman Division One South

www.hythetownfc.co.uk
Official Matchday Programme 2015/16
£2.00

**Hythe Town v Maidstone United XI**

Wednesday 29th July 2015 7.45pm

Pre-Season Friendly

www.hythetownfc.co.uk
Official Matchday Programme 2014 – 15
£1.50

# Cricklefield Stadium

◄

Programme from
Ilford v. East Ham United
28th October 1996

►

Programme from
Ilford v. Corinthian Casuals
9th December 1961

►►

Programme from
Ilford v. Grays Athletic
22nd November 1975

# Lynn Road

MEMBER OF THE FOOTBALL ASSOCIATION, LONDON F.A., ESSEX COUNTY F.A. AMATEUR FOOTBALL ALLIANCE

| SEASON | ILFORD FOOTBALL CLUB. | 1961-62 |
|---|---|---|

FOUNDED 1881

Chairman
L. G. REEVE
517, Aldborough Road, Ilford.

Hon. Treasurer
J. E. GAFFNEY,
226, Albert Road, London. E.10.

Hon. Secretary :
C. G. SAINS, B.E.M.
65, Aragon Drive, Barkingside.

Asst. Hon. Sec.
W. J. NEWMAN,
4, Eccleston Crescent,
Chadwell Heath.

President : GEO. W. DRANE, Esq

**Founding Members of The Isthmian League**

**CHAMPIONS**
1906-07,
1920-21, 1921-22.

**WINNERS :**
F.A. Amateur Cup,
1928-29, 1929-30.
Finalists—1935-36,
1957-58.

**London Senior Cup**
1900-01, 1904-05,
1913-14, 1921-22,
1928-29, 1929-30,
1953-54.

**WINNERS :**
Essex Senior Cup
1887-88, 1888-89,
1889-90, 1891-92,
1903-04, 1907-08,
1912-13, 1923-24,
1926-27, 1927-28,
1928-29, 1952-53,
1953-54.

**WINNERS :**
London Charity Cup
1921-22, 1929-30,
1937-38, 1954-55.

Thames-side Trophy
1949-50, 1954-55, 1959-60

**WINNERS :**
Guernsey Victory Cup
1934-35.

Victor Linart
Challenge Trophy
(France)

1953-54, 1954-55,
1956-57, 1957-58.

## ILFORD v. CORINTHIAN-CASUALS

TODAY we welcome the " Kennington " Casuals, who play their football in the shadow of the Oval gasometers, if the sun ever shines enough in that part of the world during the soccer season to cause a shadow.

We are out to avenge the 0—2 defeat they handed out to us the first game in November, just when we thought our luck had changed, and we had overrun Oxford City. On that occasion, as always, they played anything but casual.

Last week against Dulwich still no joy. Two goals down in the first ten minutes the boys fought back and at half-time were well in the game after a good goal from " Dickie " Winch. In the second half we had more than our fair share of the game but could not get the ball into the net even from the penalty spot. International Les Brown made certain of the Dulwich win with a further breakaway goal.

The Reserves crashed badly at Maidstone 0—7. This is no reflection on young Derek Shewring in goal who did everything expected of him on a very busy afternoon. " Ollie " Oliver was out of the side through injury and this allowed Roy Seidenbird (recently returned to us from Walthamstow) to have his first game, unfortunately out of position, at centre forward.

Alf Christmas' wrists are well on the mend, its quite an education to watch Alf lift a pint mug balanced between his two plastered arms. Whilst out of training he can manage.

January 1962 approaching, and the Great Pot Hunt in view. On the 13th we are away to Hornchurch in the Essex Senior Cup. On the 20th we have Wimbledon at home for the First Round proper of the great Wembley trail, and the following week we are home again in the London Senior Cup to Civil Service.

Dickie Winch heads our only goal against Dulwich Hamlet last week. He scored from the rebound after Roy Hammond had hit the post.

# ILFORD

Members of
**Rothmans Isthmian League**
Football Association
Essex County F.A.
London F.A.

# ILFORD v. GRAYS ATHLETIC

*Essex Professional Cup*          *Second Round*

*Saturday 22nd. November 1975*          *Kick-off 3:00 p.m.*

Official Programme 6p.

# Rockingham Road

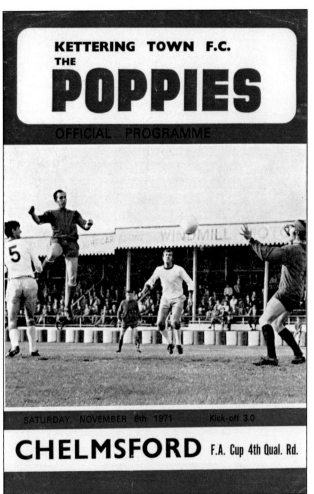

◀

Programme from
Kettering Town v. Chelmsford City
6th November 1971

▶

Programme from
Kettering Town v. Deal Town
29th August 1964

▶▶

Programme from
Kettering Town v. Hereford United
9th September 1961

# Rockingham Road

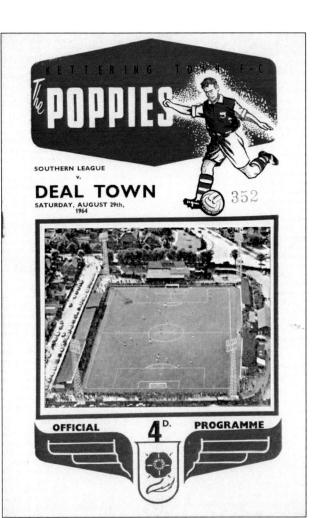

KETTERING TOWN F.C

The POPPIES

SOUTHERN LEAGUE
v.
**DEAL TOWN**
SATURDAY, AUGUST 29th,
1964

352

**OFFICIAL** 4D. **PROGRAMME**

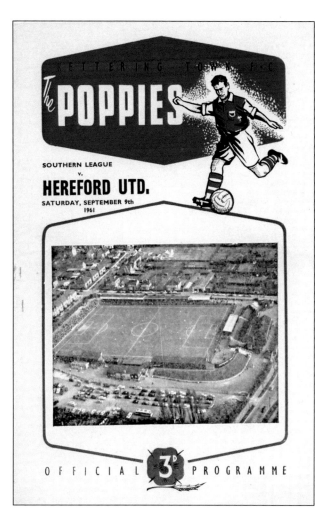

KETTERING TOWN F.C

The POPPIES

SOUTHERN LEAGUE
v.
**HEREFORD UTD.**
SATURDAY, SEPTEMBER 9th
1961

OFFICIAL 3D PROGRAMME

# Rockingham Road

KETTERING TOWN FOOTBALL CLUB

OFFICIAL PROGRAMME

WEDNESDAY, 11th APRIL 1973    Kick-off 7.30

**DOVER**

Southern League Premier Division

◄

Programme from
Kettering Town v. Dover
11th April 1973

▶

Programme from
Kettering Town v. Gravesend & Northfleet
11th April 1981

▶▶

Programme from
Kettering Town v. Yeovil Town
7th January 1984

# Rockingham Road

# KETTERING TOWN
# FOOTBALL CLUB (1950) LTD.

Southern League Champions 1927-28, 1956-57, 1972-73. Runners up 1928-29, 1978-79

Southern League Cupwinner 1974-75 F.A. Trophy Runners up 1978-79

ALLIANCE PREMIER LEAGUE

versus

# GRAVESEND & NORTHFLEET

SATURDAY 11th APRIL 1981 Kick off 3.00 p.m.

PROGRAMME 20p

**SPOT THE POPPY** 🌑 One programme has a hidden poppy (as shown) can you spot it? Winner receives a Kitbag donated by Player Sports.

# Kettering Town
## *Football Club*
### 1983-84

## Official Programme 30p

*Versus*

## YEOVIL

# Aggborough

◄

Programme from
Kidderminster Harriers v. Southport
17th February 1986

▶

Programme from
Kidderminster Harriers v. Blackburn Rovers
24th November 1979

▶▶

Programme from
Kidderminster Harriers v. Gloucester City
16th September 1974

# Aggborough

# KIDDERMINSTER
## HARRIERS
### FOOTBALL CLUB

## OFFICIAL PROGRAMME

**BILL GREAVES MEMORIAL STAND**

FIVEPENCE

# KIDDERMINSTER HARRIERS
# FOOTBALL CLUB LTD

FOUNDED 1886

**KIDDERMINSTER HARRIERS FOOTBALL CLUB LIMITED**

Members of F.A., Worcestershire F.A., Southern Football League, Border Counties League

| West Midlands Regional League Champions | | | | Birmingham League Champions | | |
| --- | --- | --- | --- | --- | --- | --- |
| 1968/69 | 1969/70 | 1970/71 | | 1937/38 | 1938/39 | 1964/65 |

| Birmingham Senior Cup Winners | | | | Worcestershire Senior Cup Winners | | |
| --- | --- | --- | --- | --- | --- | --- |
| 1933/34 | 1934/35 | 1937/38 | 1945/46 | 1936/37 | 1965/66 | 1966/67 | 1968/69 |
| 1963/64 | 1964/65 | 1966/67 | | 1970/71 | 1971/72 | 1972/73 |

| West Midlands Regional League Cup Winners | | | |
| --- | --- | --- | --- |
| 1966/67 | 1968/69 | 1969/70 | 1970/71 |

| Border Counties League Champions | | |
| --- | --- | --- |
| 1969/70 | 1970/71 | 1971/72 |

| Camkin Cup Winners | | |
| --- | --- | --- |
| 1967/68 | 1968/69 | 1969/70 |

# Culver Road

◄

Programme from
Lancing v. Hastings Town
22nd November 1989

▶

Programme from
King's Lynn v. Bexleyheath & Welling
16th December 1961

▶▶

King's Lynn v. Burton Albion
22nd April 1967

# The Walks

LANCING
FOOTBALL
CLUB

Wednesday November 22nd 1989        Kick-off 7.30 p.m.

## HASTINGS

Senior Cup                    Second Round

OFFICIAL PROGRAMME       SEASON 1989/90       PRICE 20p.

# King's Lynn FC Ltd

859

Season 1961-62

Eastern Daily Press Photo

### Saturday, December 16, 1961

2.15 p.m.

SOUTHERN LEAGUE

## BEXLEYHEATH

OFFICIAL        PROGRAMME

3D

---

# KING'S LYNN F.C. LTD

179

THE WALKS STADIUM

Season 1966-67

Lynn News & Advertiser Photo

### Saturday, April 22, 1967

3.0 p.m.

SOUTHERN LEAGUE

## BURTON ALBION

OFFICIAL        PROGRAMME

6D

◄

Programme from
Leamington v. Corby Town
18th October 1983

▶

Programme from
Kingstonian v. Woking
16th September 1989

# Kingsmeadow

▶▶

Programme from
Kingstonian v. Wokingham Town
27th November 1984

# Richmond Road

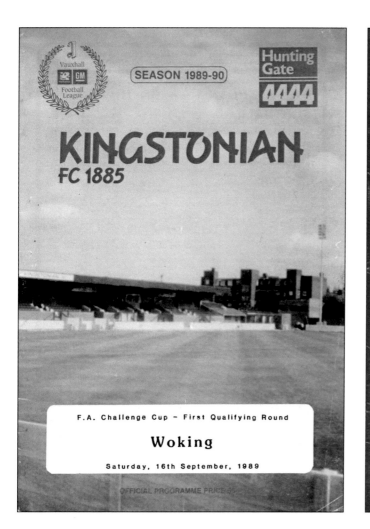

# KINGSTONIAN
## FC 1885

F.A. Challenge Cup – First Qualifying Round

## Woking

Saturday, 16th September, 1989

OFFICIAL PROGRAMME PRICE 35p

# Kingstonian
# Football Club
# (1885)

Hitachi Cup – Second Round Replay

## Wokingham Town

Tuesday, 27th November, 1984    7.30 p.m.

Official Match-Day Programme
SEASON 1984-85
Price 25p

# Baldock Road

◄

Programme from
Letchworth Garden City v. Epsom & Ewell
18th February 1978

LETCHWORTH GARDEN
CITY FOOTBALL CLUB

OFFICIAL PROGRAMME

7p

► 

Programme from
Leicester United v. Shepshed Charterhouse
20th March 1990

Programme from
Leicester United v. Dudley Town
20th October 1990

# United Park

# MATCHDAY PROGRAMME

## LEICESTER UNITED FOOTBALL CLUB

WE WELCOME TODAYS OPPONENTS

THE SOUTHERN FOOTBALL LEAGUE
Founded 1894

THE BEAZER HOMES FOOTBALL LEAGUE MIDLAND DIVISION SEASON 1989/90

50p

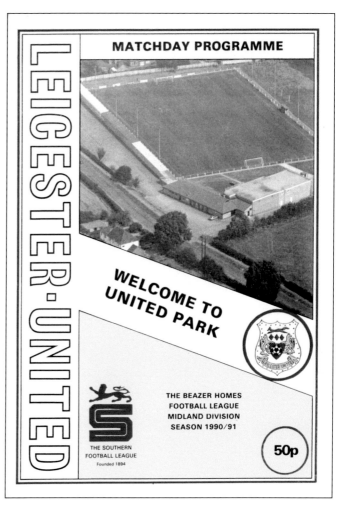

# MATCHDAY PROGRAMME

## LEICESTER · UNITED

## WELCOME TO UNITED PARK

THE SOUTHERN FOOTBALL LEAGUE
Founded 1894

THE BEAZER HOMES FOOTBALL LEAGUE MIDLAND DIVISION SEASON 1990/91

50p

1886-1986 *Stones Centenary Year*

VAUXHALL-OPEL

GM

*League*

v. FINCHLEY
Saturday 26th. April 1986
Kick-off 3.00p.m.
Vol. 7 No. 26
Official Programme 20p.

# Granleigh Road

◄

Programme from
Leytonstone Ilford v. Finchley
26th April 1986

►

Programme from
Lewes v. Aveley
6th March 1982

# The Dripping Pan

►►

Programme from
Lordswood v. Herne Bay
29th September 2001

# Martin Grove

**BERGER**
ISTHMIAN LEAGUE
DIVISION 1
Season 1981/82

# LEWES
## FOOTBALL CLUB

OFFICIAL
**15p**
PROGRAMME

SPONSORED
BY
NICO

Ground
"The Dripping Pan"
Tel: Lewes 2100

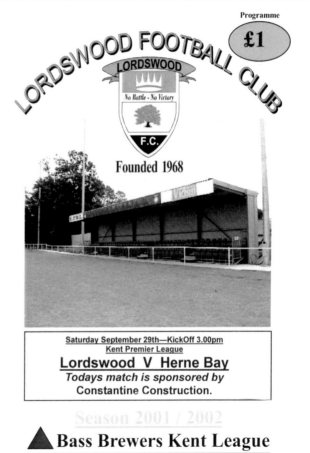

LORDSWOOD FOOTBALL CLUB

LORDSWOOD
*No Battle - No Victory*
F.C.

Founded 1968

Programme
**£1**

Saturday September 29th—KickOff 3.00pm
Kent Premier League
## Lordswood V Herne Bay
*Todays match is sponsored by*
**Constantine Construction.**

Season 2001 / 2002

▲ **Bass Brewers Kent League**

# Moss Rose

◀

Programme from
Macclesfield Town v. Stafford Rangers
27th September 1969

▶

Programme from
Maidenhead United v. Boreham Wood
9th September 1972

# York Road

▶▶

Programme from
Maidstone United v. Crockenhill
16th December 2000

# The Athletic Ground

# maidenhead united football club

OFFICIAL PROGRAMME **5p**

FOUNDED 1869

Photograph by courtesy of 'Maidenhead Advertiser'

ATHENIAN LEAGUE PREMIER DIVISION   Season 1972/73

## Maidenhead Utd. v Boreham Wood
## Saturday, SEPTEMBER 9th, 1972

KICK OFF 3 pm

---

# STONES NEWS

*British Energy*
### KENT COUNTY FOOTBALL LEAGUE
### Premier Division

## Maidstone United
## v
## Crockenhill

**OFFICIAL MATCHDAY PROGRAMME 2000/2001**
PRICE £1

Kent County League
Programme of the Year
Wirral Programme Club

1st TEAM SPONSORS
**M.I.Pankhurst Ltd**

# Cossham Street

◄

Programme from
Mangotsfield United v. Clitheroe
16th March 1996

►

Programme from
Margate v. Dartford
21st August 1978

# Hartsdown Park

►►

Programme from
Marine v. Accrington Stanley
26th July 2011

# Rossett Park

# MARGATE FOOTBALL CLUB

SEASON 1978-79 — OFFICIAL PROGRAMME 10p

FOR LEISURE AND PLEASURE

## WELCOME
### to the
### ISLE OF
### THANET

BROADSTAIRS

MARGATE

RAMSGATE ✱ WHY NOT PAY US A VISIT — SOON ✱

---

# MARINE AFC

**Matchday Programme**

£1

MARINE A.F.C. 1894

ARRIVA

Beckie-L

INTEREUROPE

**MARINE FC Vs ACCRINGTON STANLEY**

Pre-Season Friendly Sponsored by
**Corex Construction**

Tuesday 26th July — Kick Off 7:30pm
Arriva Stadium, College Rd, Crosby

# 412 Walton Road

◄

Programme from
Molesey v. Walton & Hersham
11th January 1995

►

Programme from
Marlow v. Apsley
27th November 1937

►►

Programme from
Marlow v. Wivenhoe Town
24th November 1990

# Alfred Davis
# Memorial Ground

# The Marlow Football Club

### FOUNDED 1870

## SPARTAN LEAGUE — DIVISIONS I & II

Headquarters - The Railway Hotel
Ground - The Alfred Davis Memorial Ground, Oak Tree Lane
Colours - Royal Blue and White

## OFFICIAL PROGRAMME

### PRICE ONE PENNY

*Photo by          Gorvils, Marlow*

### SEASON 1937-38

NUMBER   -   -   -

**MEN FOLK LOVE THE GAME OF FOOTBALL.**

# MARLOW FOOTBALL CLUB

## Alfred Davis Memorial Ground

### Telephone (0628) 483970

First Team Sponsor: P. E. Cole Property Maintenance  (See inside front cover)

Programme Sponsor: Platts of Marlow  (See rear cover)

## OFFICIAL PROGRAMME

### Premier Division

WIVENHOE TOWN

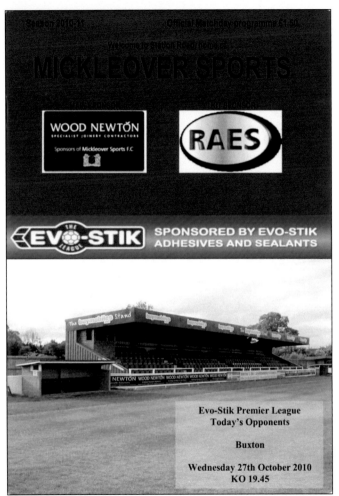

◄

Programme from
Mickleover Sports v. Buxton
27th October 2010

►

Programme from
Needham Market Reserves v. Wivenhoe Town
5th September 2015

# Bloomfields

►►

Programme from
Moor Green v. Bridgnorth Town
1st May 1986

# The Moorlands

# the marketmen

Issue 3 | **Wivenhoe Town** | Saturday 5th September 2015     Official Matchday Programme | **£2**

**Respect**

# MOOR GREEN

## FOOTBALL CLUB

### SOUTHERN LEAGUE
#### MIDLAND DIVISION

CLUB  SPONSOR

The 'MOORS' Magazine 1985/6     Price 20p

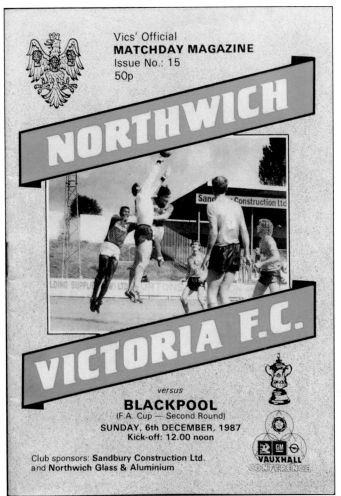

◄

Programme from
Northwich Victoria v.Blackpool
6th December 1987

▶

Programme from
Nuneaton Borough v. Folkestone
14th March 1966

# Manor Park

▶▶

Programme from
Ossett Albion v. Lancaster City
29th September 2007

# Queen's Terrace

## Southern League Premier Division

# FOLKESTONE

## Monday, March 14th

### OFFICIAL PROGRAMME 6d.

**FOOTBALL AT MANOR PARK**
Saturday, March 19th          Kick-off 3.0 p.m.
SOUTHERN LEAGUE — PREMIER DIVISION
Y E O V I L

# OSSETT ALBION
## FOOTBALL CLUB

**Club Sponsors**

*ALBION*
*V*
LANCASTER C

PAGHAM
FOOTBALL CLUB
Home of the lions

PAGHAM RESERVES
SUSSEX COUNTY FOOTBALL LEAGUE
RESERVE PREMIER
OFFICIAL PROGRAMME 2009/10

# Nyetimber Lane

◄

Programme from
Pagham Reserves v. Wick Reserves
28th October 2009

►

Programme from
Oxford City v. Hayes
18th August 1971

►►

Programme from
Oxford City v. Sutton United
31st October 1979

# White Horse Ground

By kind permission of Oxford Mail and Times

OXFORD CITY
FOOTBALL CLUB
WHITE HOUSE
GROUND

Wed., Aug. 18th, 1971
Kick-off 7.30 p.m.

ISTHMIAN LEAGUE

**OXFORD CITY** N⁰ 307

*versus*

# HAYES

Official Programme          Price 3p.

# OXFORD CITY
# FOOTBALL CLUB

CIVITAS OXONIENSIS
FORTIS EST VERITAS
Founded          1882

BERGER ISTHMIAN
LEAGUE
## 1979-80
PREMIER DIVISION

OFFICIAL
PROGRAMME
## 10p

**POLYTECHNIC FOOTBALL CLUB**

(Founded 1875)

Headquarters: THE POLYTECHNIC, 309, REGENT STREET, W.1 (Langham 2020)

President—
THE Rt. Hon.
THE VISCOUNT HAILSHAM

Hon. Secretary—
E. GALVIN

Members of the Football Association, The Spartan League (Premier Division)
Affiliated to the London Football Association, Middlesex County F.A. and Amateur Football Alliance

Ground: POLYTECHNIC STADIUM, HARTINGTON ROAD
CHISWICK, W.4 (Chiswick 5817)

**OFFICIAL PROGRAMME** - Price 2d.

# Polytechnic Stadium

◀

Programme from
Polytechnic v. Harrow Town
1st November 1952

▶

Programme from
Paulton Rovers v. Taunton Town
9th April 1994

# Athletic Field

▶▶

Programme from
Pershore Town v. Nuneaton Griff
9th October 2010

# King George V Playing Fields

Founded in 1881

# PAULTON ROVERS
## A.F.C.

*versus*

### TAUNTON TOWN

Saturday, 9th April 1994
Kick off 3.00pm

SEASON
1993 – 94

**GREAT MILLS LEAGUE**
**PREMIER DIVISION**
**and SOMERSET SENIOR LEAGUE**

OFFICIAL
PROGRAMME
30p

MAIN SPONSOR

**DESIGN WINDOWS**

PERSHORE TOWN F.C.

OFFICIAL MATCH DAY PROGRAMME

*Season 2010-2011*

# Church Road

◄

Programme from
Portfield v. Little Common Albion
26th October 1991

►

Programme from
Poole Town v. Nuneaton Borough
13th February 1960

►►

Programme from
Poole Town v. Wellington Town
22nd January 1966

# The Stadium

# POOLE TOWN F.C.

THE STADIUM - POOLE     Telephone : POOLE 790

Aerial View of Poole Stadium

Saturday, February 13th, 1960

**POOLE TOWN**

v

# NUNEATON

Southern League Premier Div.     Kick-off 3.0 p.m.

PROGRAMME                              LUCKY NUMBER
3d.

This Programme is Published by the Supporters' Club.
Designed and Printed by The Ashley Press, 8, Sherwood Avenue, Parkstone, Poole.  Tel.—Parkstone 3239.

# POOLE TOWN F.C.

v

# WELLINGTON TOWN

Southern League Premier Div.     Kick-off 3.0 p.m.

Saturday, January 22nd, 1966

**6**D.

LUCKY NUMBER    301

This Programme is Published by The Supporters' Club.
Printed by The Ashley Press, 8 Sherwood Avenue, Parkstone, Poole. Tel. Parkstone 3239

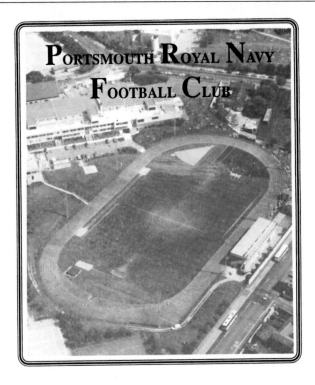

PORTSMOUTH ROYAL NAVY
FOOTBALL CLUB

*JEWSON Wessex League*

**Portsmouth Royal Navy**
v
**Gosport Borough**

Monday 11 Oct 1993

# Navy Stadium

◄

Programme from
Portsmouth R. N. v. Gosport Borough
11th October 1993

►

Programme from
Raunds Town v. Ashford Town
5th February 2000

# Kiln Park

►

Programme from
Rainworth Miners' Welfare v. Pickering Town
24th March 2009

# The Welfare Ground

# Raunds Town F.C.

Kiln Park,
London Road,
Raunds,
Northamptonshire
NN9 6EQ
Tel: 01933 623351

**Dr. AirWair Martens**

**FOOTBALL
LEAGUE**

*Dr Martens Football League
Eastern Division*

**Raunds Town**
-v-
**Ashford Town**

Saturday 5th February 2000
Kick Off 3.00pm

*Programme - £1.00*

---

# The Wren

## Rainworth Miners' Welfare FC

Members of the
Koolsport Northern
Counties East
Football League
Division One

**Tuesday, 24th March
v PICKERING TOWN**
*League Cup round III*
*Today's match kindly sponsored by*
**AJ Specialist Welding Ltd**

◀

Programme from
Rolls-Royce Welfare v. Eastwood Town
17th March 1990

▶

Programme from
Ramsgate v. Maidstone United
3rd March 2012

▶▶

Programme from
Ramsgate v. Sevenoaks Town
9th August 2003

# Southwood Stadium

# Ramsgate F.C

## 2011-12
### Official Matchday Programme
www.ramsgate-fc.co.uk
Ramsgate Football Club (85) Limited - Reg No 02077612

*truprint* media

**Main Club Sponsors**

AIRPORT CONNECTIONS | CARDY

Respect
Ryman
*football league*

TODAYS VISITORS
**MAIDSTONE UNITED**

---

# RAMSGATE Football Club

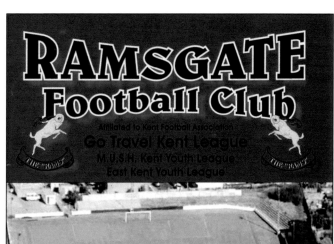

Affiliated to Kent Football Association
**Go Travel Kent League**
M.U.S.H. Kent Youth League
East Kent Youth League

**Main Club Sponsor**

**Thanet Waste Management**
SKIP HIRE: 2,3,4,6,8,9,10,12 cu. Yd.
CONTAINER HIRE: 15,20,25,35,40,50 cu. Yd.
Manston Road, Margate, Kent CT9 4JW
Tel: 01843 821500    Fax: 01843 821504

**WELCOME TO SOUTHWOOD FOOTBALL STADIUM**

**SEVENOAKS TOWN F. C.**

Saturday 9th August 2003    **OFFICIAL MATCH PROGRAMME**

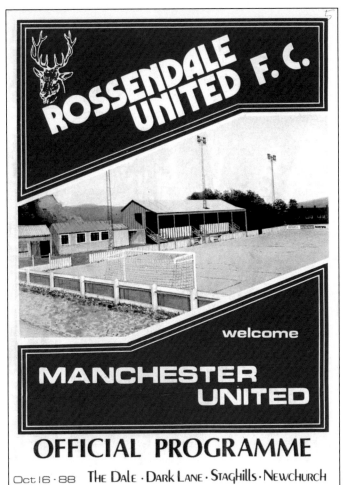

◄

Programme from
Rossendale United v. Manchester United
16th October 1988

►

Programme from
Redhill v. Leatherhead
20th August 1968

►►

Programme from
Redhill v. Maidenhead United
5th April 1969

# The Memorial Ground

# REDHILL
## Football Club

**SEASON 1968 - 1969**

FOUNDED 1894    Programme 6d.

*MEMBERS OF*

The Football Association
The Surrey County Football Association
The Athenian League ; The Premier Midweek Floodlit League
The Surrey Combination Youth League
The Redhill and District Football League (Minor)

**THE MEMORIAL SPORTS GROUND, LONDON ROAD
REDHILL, SURREY (TELEPHONE : REDHILL 62129)**

Colours : Red and White    Alternative Colours : Blue and White

# REDHILL
## Football Club

**SEASON 1968 - 1969**

FOUNDED 1894    Programme 6d.

*MEMBERS OF*

The Football Association
The Surrey County Football Association
The Athenian League ; The Premier Midweek Floodlit League
The Surrey Combination Youth League
The Redhill and District Football League (Minor)

**THE MEMORIAL SPORTS GROUND, LONDON ROAD
REDHILL, SURREY (TELEPHONE : REDHILL 62129)**

Colours : Red and White    Alternative Colours : Blue and White

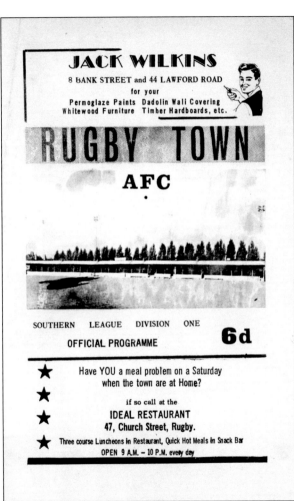

JACK WILKINS

8 BANK STREET and 44 LAWFORD ROAD

for your

Permoglaze Paints  Dadolin Wall Covering
Whitewood Furniture  Timber Hardboards, etc.

# RUGBY TOWN

## AFC

SOUTHERN  LEAGUE  DIVISION  ONE

OFFICIAL PROGRAMME      **6d**

★  Have YOU a meal problem on a Saturday
★  when the town are at Home?
★  if so call at the
   **IDEAL RESTAURANT**
★  47, Church Street, Rugby.
   Three course Luncheons in Restaurant, Quick Hot Meals in Snack Bar
   OPEN 9 A.M. – 10 P.M. every day

# Oakfield

◄

Programme from
Rugby Town v. Ashford Town
10th December 1966

►

Programme from
Romford v. Rugby Town
10th November 1962

►►

Programme from
Romford v. Bexleyheath & Welling
23rd March 1963

# Brooklands

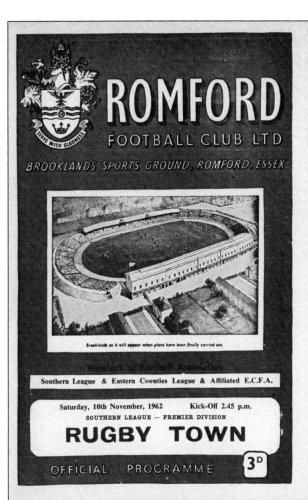

**ROMFORD**
FOOTBALL CLUB LTD

BROOKLANDS SPORTS GROUND, ROMFORD, ESSEX

*Brooklands as it will appear when plans have been finally carried out.*

Members of Football Association

Southern League & Eastern Counties League & Affiliated E.C.F.A.

Saturday, 10th November, 1962    Kick-Off 2.45 p.m.
SOUTHERN LEAGUE — PREMIER DIVISION

# RUGBY TOWN

OFFICIAL PROGRAMME    3D

**ROMFORD**
FOOTBALL CLUB LTD

BROOKLANDS SPORTS GROUND, ROMFORD, ESSEX

Members of Football Association

Southern League & Eastern Counties League & Affiliated E.C.F.A.

Saturday, 23rd March, 1963    Kick-Off 3 p.m.
SOUTHERN LEAGUE — PREMIER DIVISION

# BEXLEYHEATH & WELLING

OFFICIAL PROGRAMME    3D

RUISLIP FOOTBALL CLUB LTD.

The
BEAZER HOMES
LEAGUE
(SOUTHERN SECTION)

Official Matchday Programme
Season 1988~89
30p

# Breakspear Road

◄

Programme from
Ruislip v. Crockenhill
3rd September 1988

►

Programme from
Royston Town v. Biggleswade Town
24th August 1999

# Garden Walk

# The Crows

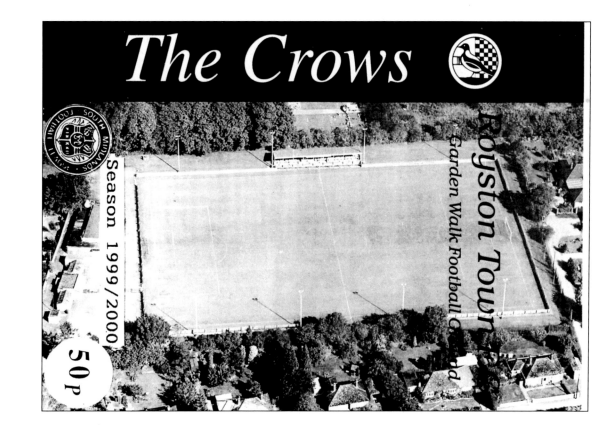

Royston Town

Garden Walk Football Ground

Season 1999/2000

50p

# Canal Street

◀

Programme from
Runcorn v. Northwich Victoria
5th December 1964

▶

Programme from
Saffron Walden Town v. Whitton United
19th February 2005

# Catons Lane

▶▶

Programme from
Scarborough v. Enfield
15th September 1984

# Seamer Road

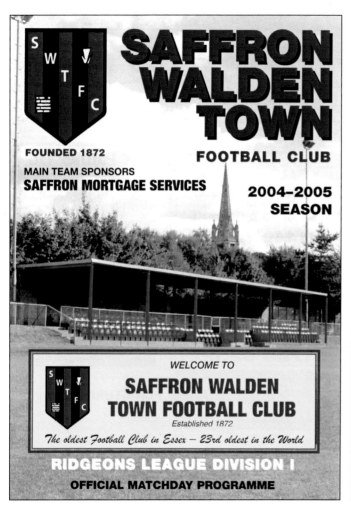

# Botany Road

◄

Programme from
Sheppey United v. Canterbury City
22nd September 1987

►

Programme from
Shepshed Charterhouse v. Morecambe
8th October 1988

# The Dovecote

►►

Programme from
Shifnal Town v. Leamington
23rd April 2005

# Phoenix Park

## SHEPSHED CHARTERHOUSE

FOOTBALL CLUB LTD.          SEASON 1988/9

 "THE RAIDERS"

OFFICIAL MATCH PROGRAMME 30p

# SHIFNAL TOWN FOOTBALL CLUB

CLUB SPONSORS
SmartWater Technology
(Europe) Ltd

midland football combination premier division

# Dean Street

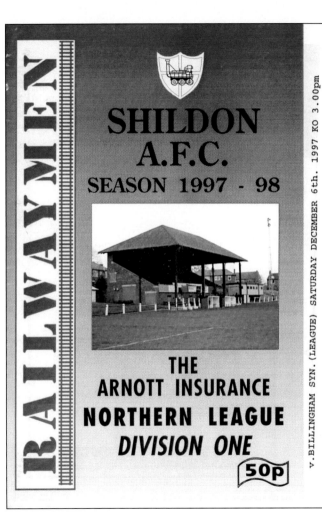

◄

Programme from
Shildon v. Billingham Synthonia
6th December 1997

►

Programme from
Sittingbourne v. Ashford Town
23rd October 2001

# Central Park

►►

Programme from
Smethwick Highfield v. Walsall Borough
March 1985
No precise date was included in the programme

# The Sports Centre

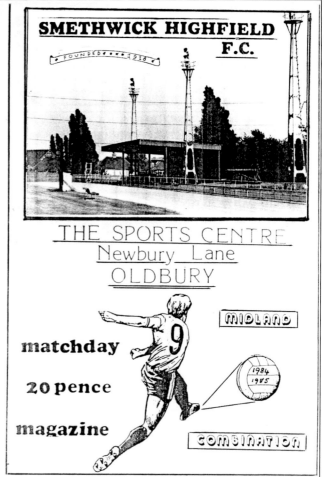

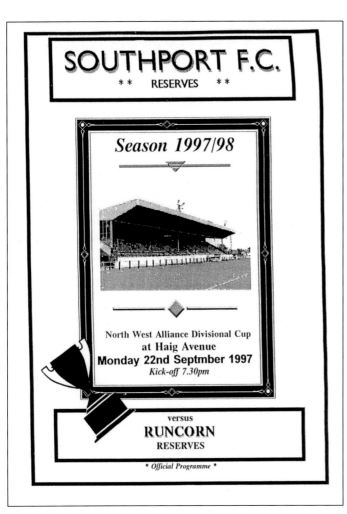

◄

Programme from
Southport Reserves v. Runcorn Reserves
22nd September 1997

►

Programme from
Slough Town v. Leyton
5th May 1968

►►

Programme from
Slough Town v. Leytonstone
28th October 1967

# The Dolphin Stadium

# SLOUGH TOWN FOOTBALL CLUB

### FOUNDED 1890

## OFFICIAL PROGRAMME    PRICE 6d.

# SLOUGH TOWN FOOTBALL CLUB

### FOUNDED 1890

## OFFICIAL PROGRAMME
### OCTOBER 28th 1967

# Clarence Park

◄
Programme from
St. Albans City v. Hendon
17th April 1974

►
Programme from
Slough Town v. Witton Albion
2nd November 1991

►►
Programme from
Slough Town v. Billericay Town
11th February 1984

# Wexham Park Stadium

# Slough Town

OFFICIAL MATCH
PROGRAMME

By courtesy of Slough Express

GM VAUXHALL CONFERENCE

## Witton Albion

Saturday 2nd November 1991  Kick off 3.00pm

Main Sponsor UK Parcels

GM VAUXHALL
CONFERENCE

80p

# SLOUGH TOWN
# FOOTBALL CLUB

## SERVOWARM ISTHMIAN LEAGUE

SEASON
## 1983~4

OFFICIAL
MATCH
PROGRAMME

WEXHAM
PARK
STADIUM
SLOUGH
BERKS

PROGRAMME
## 25p

v
Billericay
Town

◀

Programme from
St Blazey v. Swindon Supermarine
23rd October 1999

▶

Programme from
South Liverpool v. Runcorn
6th December 1969

Programme from
South Liverpool v. Mossley
18th October 1983

# Holly Park

## Official Programme

### South Liverpool Football Club Co. Ltd.

Photograph by courtesy of "Liverpool Weekly News."

## Holly Park, Garston, Liverpool, 19.

### NORTHERN PREMIER LEAGUE
### SOUTH LIVERPOOL
### V.
# RUNCORN
### Saturday, 6th December, 1969
### Kick-off 3-0 p.m.

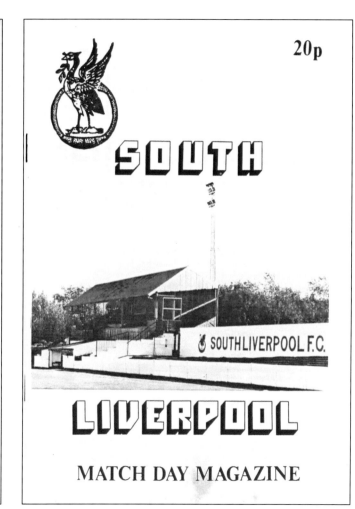

20p

# SOUTH
# LIVERPOOL

## MATCH DAY MAGAZINE

*Join the Boro' Social Club*

STAFFORD RANGERS
F.C. LTD.

(FOUNDED 1876)                    *Photographed by PETER ROGERS*

GROUND:- MARSTON ROAD, STAFFORD
Telephone: Stafford 2750

BORO' SOCIAL CLUB
Telephone: Stafford 52284

Members of
NORTHERN PREMIER LEAGUE
and
MIDLAND FLOODLIT CUP COMPETITION

Colours    BLACK AND WHITE

Manager    R. CHAPMAN

CLUB OFFICIALS

President       Dr. H. Simon, D. Eng. Chem. M. Inst. B.E.
Chairman        Mr. P. T. W. Butters
Vice-Chairman   Mr. R. N. Heath
Directors       Mr. C. H. Jones,   Mr. S. J. E. Richards
                Mr. R. Butters,  Mr. G. D. Swinton,
                Mr. K. A. Wainwright

Company      Mr. R. F. PEPPER        OFFICIAL PROGRAMME    Match      Mr. F. W. TUNNICLIFFE
Secretary:   12 CLEVEDON AVENUE                           Secretary  206 SANDON ROAD
             STAFFORD                    SIXPENCE                     STAFFORD
             Telephone: Home 61424                                   Telephone : Home 53363
                        Office 2839                                             Ground 2750

# Marston Road

◄

Programme from
Stafford Rangers v. Kirkby Town
30th September 1970

►

Programme from
South Shields v. Billingham Synthonia
15th October 1966

►►

Programme from
South Shields v. Consett
9th March 1963

# Simonside Hall

OFFICIAL PROGRAMME
PRICE 3d.
# SOUTH SHIELDS
## ASSOCIATION FOOTBALL CLUB Ltd.
SIMONSIDE HALL                 Season 1966 — 67

**F.A. CUP    4th Qualifying Round**
Saturday, October 15th, 1966     Kick-off 3-0 p.m.
Today's
Visitors **BILLINGHAM Synthonia**

## LEWIS BOTTO LIMITED
### 100 CLAYTON STREET
### JARROW, Co. Durham.
Tel: Jarrow 898371

---

OFFICIAL PROGRAMME
PRICE 2d.                 Nᵒ 64
# SOUTH SHIELDS
## ASSOCIATION FOOTBALL CLUB Ltd.
SIMONSIDE HALL

**DURHAM CHALLENGE CUP**
Saturday, March 9th, 1963  Kick-off 3-0 p.m.
Today's
Visitors **CONSETT**
WON 6-4

## LEWIS BOTTO LIMITED
### 100 CLAYTON STREET
### JARROW, Co. Durham.
Tel: Jarrow 898371

◀

Programme from
Stamford v. Newport Pagnell Town
24th October 1992

▶

Programme from
Stamford v. Buxton
26th September 1998

# Wothorpe Road

Season
1998-99

# STAMFORD A.F.C.

## OFFICIAL PROGRAMME

Dr. AirWair
Martens
Bouncing

FOOTBALL

LEAGUE

It's GROVES Draught Beer
in our Social Club!!

Groves & Whitnall Ltd. · Regent Road Brewery · Salford 5

*(a Member of the Greenall Whitley Group)*

# Bower Fold

◀

Programme from
Stalybridge Celtic v. Horwich R.M.I.
10th April 1971

▶

Programme from
Stowmarket Town v. Wisbech Town
19th April 1995

# Greens Meadow

▶▶

Programme from
Sudbury Town v. Bury Town
18th April 1992

# Priory Stadium

## THE JEWSON LEAGUE

# STOWMARKET TOWN FOOTBALL CLUB

## OFFICIAL MATCHDAY MAGAZINE 1994/95

### Welcome to GREENS MEADOWS

*Team Sponsors: "STANNARDS"*

### The Goldliner 30p

PRODUCTION

# SUDBURY TOWN FOOTBALL CLUB

Beazer Homes League

## PRIORY STADIUM
## TEL: 79095

JEWSON FOOTBALL LEAGUE

Wheelers MAIN SPONSORS

# Wheelers
### Timber & Builders' Merchants

v. BURY TOWN
18.4.92 B.H.L.
50p

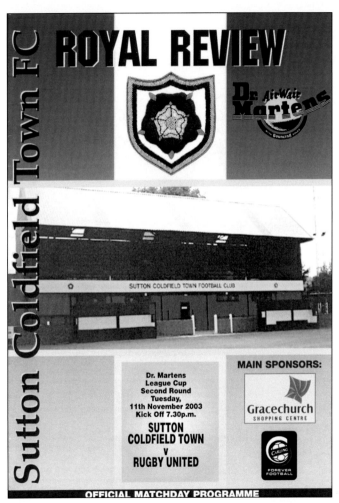

# Coles Lane

◀

Programme from
Sutton Coldfield Town v. Rugby United
11th November 2003

▶

Programme from
Taunton Town v. Welton Rovers
15th February 1993

# Wordsworth Drive

▶▶

Programme from
Tooting & Mitcham United v. Bognor Regis Town
23rd April 1985

# Sandy Lane

GREAT MILLS
**LEAGUE**
PREMIER DIVISION

# TAUNTON TOWN
## FOOTBALL CLUB

MAIN SPONSOR
STELLA ARTOIS

NEWSLINE
0891 122 901

LEAGUE CENTENARY
SEASON 1992-1993

# TOOTING & MITCHAM
# UNITED
# FOOTBALL CLUB

## Official Programme
## **20** pence

# Frome Road

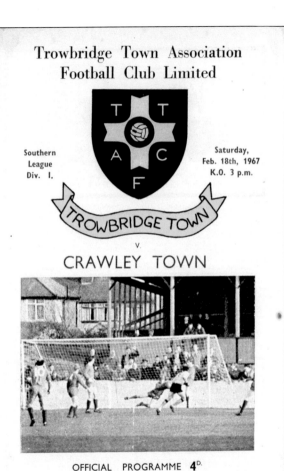

◄

Programme from
Trowbridge Town v. Crawley Town
18th February 1967

►

Programme from
Thorne Colliery v. Newark Town
14th April 2006

# The Welfare Ground

►►

Programme from
Telford United v. Kettering Town
13th December 1988

# Bucks Head

# Thorne Colliery  Football Club

FORMED 1929

OFFICIAL PROGRAMME

---

Members of the

VAUXHALL CONFERENCE

# TELFORD UTD
## FOOTBALL CLUB LIMITED

OFFICIAL PROGRAMME
FOR THE 1988/89 SEASON

50p

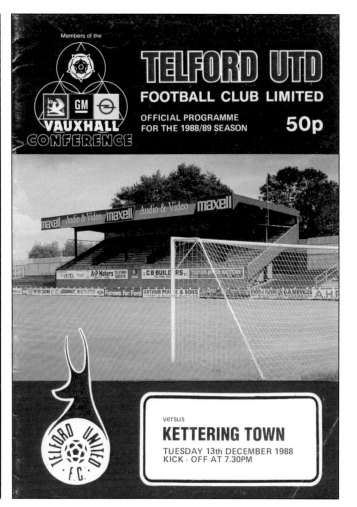

versus

## KETTERING TOWN

TUESDAY 13th DECEMBER 1988
KICK - OFF AT 7.30PM

WINSTONLEAD KENT LEAGUE DIVISION ONE 1994-1995

# TUNBRIDGE WELLS

# FOOTBALL CLUB

*(Affiliated to KCFA)*

Chairman: R J Bonny
Secretary: Peter Wager 46 Mereworth Road
Tunbridge Wells. Phone 524182
Treasurer: Shirley Brown
Manager: Mark Higgs
Coach: Tony Atkins
Honours: Kent Snr. Trophy Runners Up 1985/86, 91/92
Kent League Champions 1984/85
Kent League Runners Up 1968/69
Kent League Cup Winners 1974/75, 1977/78
1985/86, 1987/88

30p OFFICIAL PROGRAMME

**Culverden Stadium**
Telephone: 520517

◄

Programme from
Tunbridge Wells v. Furness
22nd October 1994

►

Tonbridge Handbook
1971-2

# The Angel Ground

►►

Programme from
Tonbridge Angels v. Yate Town
15th October 1994

# Longmead Stadium

# TONBRIDGE
# FOOTBALL CLUB

YEAR BOOK 1971-72

**25 Pence**

TODAY'S OPPONENTS
Yate Town F.C.
15th Oct 1994
Southern League

# Honeycroft

Programme from
Uxbridge v. Harefield United
30th March 1982

Programme from
Ilford v. Maidstone United
2nd May 1963
Photo from the previous game, played at Walthamstow Avenue

▶▶
Programme from
Walthamstow Avenue v. Bognor Regis Town
27th August 1984

# Green Pond Road

**FOUNDED 1881**

# ILFORD FOOTBALL CLUB
FOUNDER MEMBERS OF THE ISTHMIAN LEAGUE

| Chairman: | Hon. Treasurer: | Hon. Secretary: |
|---|---|---|
| L. G. REEVE, Esq. | J. E. GAFFNEY, | C. G. SAINS, B.E.M. |
| PHONE : SEVEN KINGS 1237 | 62 NETLEY ROAD, ILFORD | 65 ARAGON DRIVE, BARKINGSIDE |
| | | PHONE : HAINAULT 2633 |

**SEASON 1962-63**

Members of the Football Association, London FA, Essex County FA, Amateur Football Alliance

Ground—Newbury Park. Phone VALentine 2916       Hon. Asst. Sec. W. J. Newman, Esq. Seven Kings 7264

| Thursday, May 2nd | ISTHMIAN LEAGUE | Kick-off 7.30 p.m. |
|---|---|---|

## ILFORD v MAIDSTONE UNITED

An incident during our game against the "Avenue" last week when we
succeeded in bringing off the "double" for the first time in "modern" history.

Welcome to the men of the "Hop Growing County." Here's looking forward to a good game, with our boys out to prove that the 6-3 shaking you handed out to us when last we visited Maidstone was only lent. There are a couple of valuable points at stake tonight which we will both be well after.

These notes had to be penned before last Saturdays Second Leg of the Essex Cup Final against Barking so at the moment we don't know the outcome of the "The battle of the Creek."

We are "at home" to Tooting for the Semi-final of the London Charity Cup. Don't know when. The F.A. have now given permission for charity games to be played in June . . . who's for tennis?

# WALTHAMSTOW AVENUE F.C.

## SERVOWARM ISTHMIAN PREMIER DIVISION

v.
Bognor Regis Town
27th August, 1984.

◀

Programme from
Ware v. Dorking Town
19th March 1983

▶

Programme from
Walton & Hersham v. Crawley Town
2nd April 1968

# Stompond Lane

▶▶

Programme from
Welling United v. Wycombe Wanderes
2nd January 1993

# Park View Road

# Walton & Hersham
# Football Club

F.A. Amateur Cup—Semi-finalists 1951-52, 52-53
Corinthian League—Champions 1946-47, 47-48, 48-49; Runners-up 1949-50
Athenian League—Runners-up 1950-51
Surrey Combination Cup—Winners 1949-50
Surrey Senior Cup—Winners 1947-48, 50-51, 60-61, 61-62; Finalists 1946-47, 51-52, 59-60

PREMIER MIDWEEK FLOODLIT LEAGUE

**Tuesday, 2nd April, 1968**    **Kick-off 7.30 p.m.**

### WALTON & HERSHAM

V

### CRAWLEY TOWN

Official Programme    Price 6d.

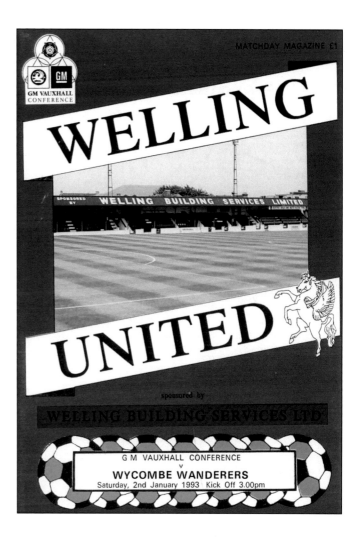

GM VAUXHALL CONFERENCE

**WELLING**

**UNITED**

sponsored by

WELLING BUILDING SERVICES LTD

G M VAUXHALL CONFERENCE
v
**WYCOMBE WANDERERS**
Saturday, 2nd January 1993 · Kick Off 3.00pm

## WESTON-SUPER-MARE FOOTBALL CLUB LTD

Great Mills League
Somerset Senior League

Telephone:
W-S-M 21618

### WOODSPRING PARK, WINTERSTOKE ROAD

**SPONSORED BY WESTON MERCURY**

WESTERN LGE. RUNNERS UP 1976/77
WESTERN LGE. K.O. CUP WINNERS 1976/77
WESTERN LGE. MERIT CUP WINNERS 1976/77 1977/78
WESTON SENIOR CUP WINNERS 1973/74/75/76 &78
RUNNERS UP WESTERN LGE. GOLDLINER CUP 1980/81
SOMERSET SENIOR LGE. DIV. 3 CHAMPIONS 1984/85
SOMERSET SENIOR LGE. DIV. 2 RUNNERS UP 1985/86

OFFICIAL PROGRAMME
**20**p
0533

◄

Programme from
Weston-Super-Mare v. Taunton Town
10th February 1987

►

Programme from
Merthyr Tydfil v. Ashford Town
15th April 1989
Action photo is from a game at Waterlooville

►►

Programme from both
Waterlooville v. Hastings United
27th December 1980

# Jubilee Park

Official Match Day Magazine 50p

CLUB SPONSORS
**HOOVER PLC**

BEAZER HOMES LEAGUE
PREMIER DIVISION

# Merthyr Tydfil
v
# AshfordTown

PENYDARREN PARK
SATURDAY, 15th APRIL, 1989
Kick off 3 p.m.

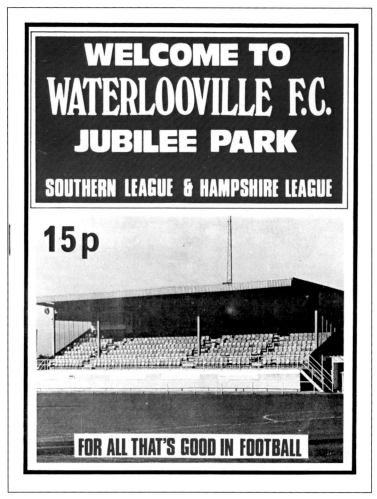

WELCOME TO
WATERLOOVILLE F.C.
JUBILEE PARK

SOUTHERN LEAGUE & HAMPSHIRE LEAGUE

15p

FOR ALL THAT'S GOOD IN FOOTBALL

**WHICKHAM F.C.**

MEMBERS OF THE SKILL TRAINING Ltd NORTHERN LEAGUE

HONOURS: FA VASE WINNERS 1980/81
FA VASE SEMI FINALS 1978/79 1983/84
DURHAM CHALLENGE CUP WINNERS 2005/06
ERNEST ARMSTRONG MEMORIAL CUP WINNERS 2006/07

GLEBE GROUND, RECTORY LANE, WHICKHAM, TYNE & WEAR

skilltraining      skilltraining

PROUDLY SPONSORED BY

**WESTERHOPE TILE CENTRE**

WHICKHAM FOOTBALL CLUB OFFICIAL MATCH DAY PROGRAMME

◄

Programme from
Whickham v. Team Northumbria
11th April 2011

►

Programme from
Wealdstone v. Gateshead
1st September 1984

►►

Programme from both
Wealdstone v. Bangor City 18th October 1980
& Gravesend & Northfleet 20th October 1980

# Lower Mead

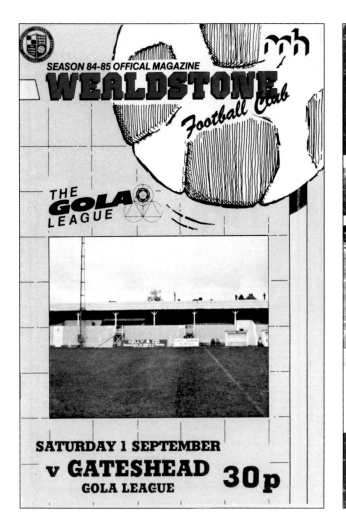

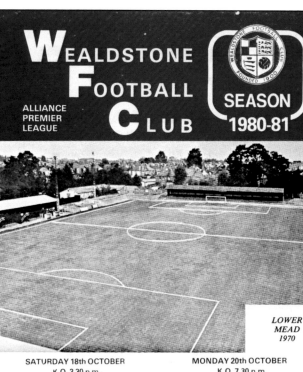

◄

Programme from
Wellington Town v. Wimbledon
26th August 1967

►

Programme from
Wellington Town v. Wimbledon
11th February 1967

►►

Programme from
Wellington Town v. Corby Town
7th November 1966

# Buck's Head

### 1966 **Wellington Town** Football Club Ltd 1967

President: J. T. STONE, ESQ.

MEMBERS OF
**FOOTBALL ASSOCIATION
SOUTHERN FOOTBALL LEAGUE
SHROPSHIRE COUNTY LEAGUE
THE MIDLAND FLOODLIT LEAGUE
CUP COMPETITION**

Birmingham League Champions—1920-21, 1934-35, 1935-36
Cheshire League Champions—1945-46, 1946-47, 1951-52
Edward Case Cup Winners—1952-53, 1954-55
Welsh Cup Winners—1901-02, 1905-06, 1939-40
Birmingham Senior Cup Winners—1946-47
Walsall Senior Cup Winners—1946-47
Birmingham League Challenge Cup Winners—1946-47
Shropshire Senior Cup—Winners 22 times

*Club Colours*—**White Shirts, White Shorts**

*Floodlit Colours*—**Red Shirts, White Shorts**

## OFFICIAL PROGRAMME - - - 6d.

### 1966 **Wellington Town** Football Club Ltd 1967

President: J. T. STONE, ESQ.

Reproduced by permission of the Shropshire Star

MEMBERS OF
**FOOTBALL ASSOCIATION
SOUTHERN FOOTBALL LEAGUE
SHROPSHIRE COUNTY LEAGUE
THE MIDLAND FLOODLIT LEAGUE
CUP COMPETITION**

Birmingham League Champions—1920-21, 1934-35, 1935-36
Cheshire League Champions—1945-46, 1946-47, 1951-52
Edward Case Cup Winners—1952-53, 1954-55
Welsh Cup Winners—1901-02, 1905-06, 1939-40
Birmingham Senior Cup Winners—1946-47
Walsall Senior Cup Winners—1946-47
Birmingham League Challenge Cup Winners—1946-47
Shropshire Senior Cup—Winners 22 times

*Club Colours*—**White Shirts, White Shorts**

*Floodlit Colours*—**Red Shirts, White Shorts**

## OFFICIAL PROGRAMME - - - 6d.

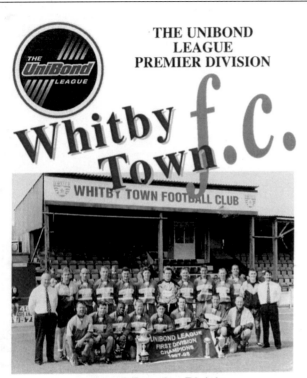

◄

Programme from
Whitby Town v. Spennymoor United
24th April 1999

►

Programme from
Weymouth v. Millwall
17th November 1984

# Recreation Ground

►►

Programme from
Weymouth v. Bath City
18th October 1989

# Wessex Stadium

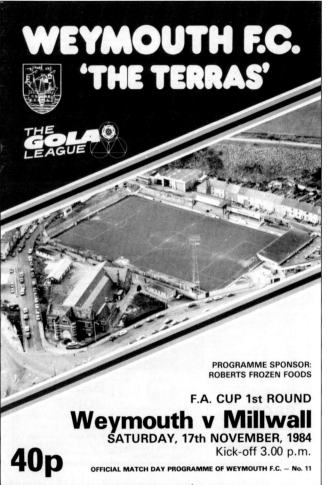

# WEYMOUTH F.C.
## 'THE TERRAS'

THE **GOLA** LEAGUE

PROGRAMME SPONSOR:
ROBERTS FROZEN FOODS

### F.A. CUP 1st ROUND
# Weymouth v Millwall
SATURDAY, 17th NOVEMBER, 1984
Kick-off 3.00 p.m.

## 40p

OFFICIAL MATCH DAY PROGRAMME OF WEYMOUTH F.C. — No. 11

---

# The *Terra-Cotta*

OFFICIAL MATCHDAY MAGAZINE OF WEYMOUTH FOOTBALL CLUB 1989/90

**Beazer Homes League**
PREMIER DIVISION

**Wednesday 18th October**
v
# BATH CITY F.C.
**Westgate Insurance Cup**
Kick Off 7.30 p.m.

Programme No. 8

## 50p

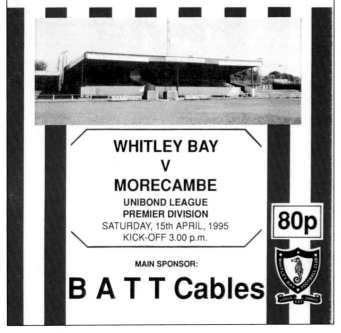

# Hillheads Park

◄

Programme from
Whitley Bay v. Morecambe
15th April 1995

►

Programme from
Whitstable Town v. Crockenhill
15th January 1994

# The Belmont Ground

►►

Programme from
Wigan Athletic v. Great Harwood
1st February 1969

# Springfield Park

CLUB SPONSOR
D & J TYRES
KIT SPONSOR
SCREEN MACHINE

WHITSTABLE TOWN F.C.

TOWN TALK

THE BELMONT GROUND

**TODAYS MATCH**

Winstonlead Kent League
v. CROCKENHILL
Sat. 15th Jan. K.O. 3·00

SEASON
93-94

# Wigan Athletic
*v.*
# Great HARWOOD

LANCASHIRE JUNIOR CUP — SECOND ROUND

*Official Programme*
*Price 9d.*

№   58

# Noose Lane

◀

Programme from
Willenhall Town v. Folkestone
5th April 1986

▶

Programme from
Wincanton Town v. Sturminster Newton
20th September 2008

# Moor Lane

▶▶

Programme from
Winterton Rovers v. Harrogate Railway
11th March 1995

# West Street

# Wincanton Town F.C

## Season 2008 / 09

### DORSET PREMIER LEAGUE
### DORSET RESERVE LEAGUE
### DORSET YOUTH LEAGUE DIVISION 1

BLACKACRE FARM EGGS

OFFICIAL MATCHDAY PROGRAMME £1

# WINTERTON RANGERS

## • FOOTBALL CLUB •

*Official Match Programme*

*50p*

**WINDSOR & ETON F.C.**
**Stag Meadow**

WINDSOR ROYALISTS

**VAUXHALL-OPEL** ——— Premier Division

*League*

★★★ Today's Match ★★★★★

dry

/alsh, F.
Oriscoll.

BERKS & BUCKS CUP
SLOUGH TOWN
30p

**Official Programme**

◄

Programme from
Windsor & Eton v. Slough Town
12th November 1985

►

Programme from
Windsor & Eton v. St. Albans City
5th December 1992

**Stag Meadow**

*Welcome to Stag Meadow*

# Windsor & Eton FC *The Royalists*

100

Main Club Sponsor

WINDSOR ROYALISTS

Centenary Season

The Diadora Football League

SATURDAY, 5TH DECEMBER 1992   OFFICIAL PROGRAMME 80 PENCE   ISSUE 11
WINDSOR & ETON v ST.ALBANS CITY   DIADORA LEAGUE PREMIER DIVISION

*Season 1992-93*

# New Manor Ground

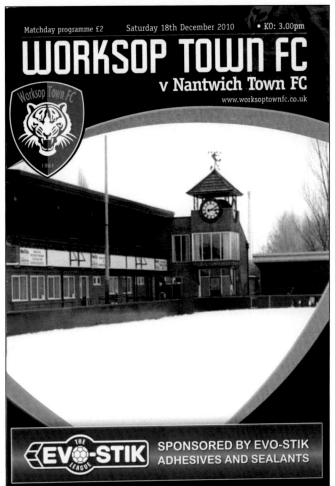

◄

Programme from
Worksop Town v. Nantwich Town
18th December 2010
The game was played at the home of Ilkeston F.C.

►

Programme from
Wivenhoe Town v. Hungerford Town
3rd January 2000

Wivenhoe Town Yearbook 1986/7

# Broad Lane

Ryman
Football League

# WIVENHOE
# TOWN F.C.

Wivenhoe Town F.C.

## 1999/2000 SEASON

£1

*VERSUS*
**HUNGERFORD TOWN**
MONDAY 3RD JANUARY 2000
RYMAN LEAGUE DIVISION TWO

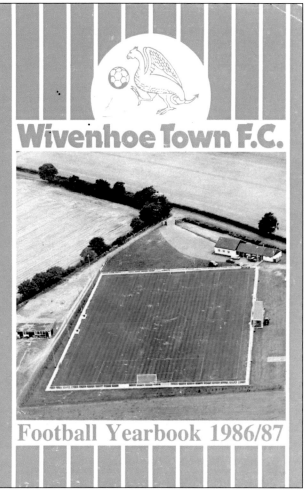

## Wivenhoe Town F.C.

### Football Yearbook 1986/87

◄

Programme from
Worcester City v. Northwich Victoria
22nd December 1984

►

Programme from
Worcester City v. Hereford United
20th October 1962

►►

Programme from
Worcester City v. Hinckley Athletic
14th November 1963

# St George's Lane

OFFICIAL PROGRAMME                                    Price 4d

# WORCESTER CITY F.C.
### LTD.

ST. GEORGE'S LANE    -    -    WORCESTER
Tel.: 25427

President: Mr. Peter Walker, M.B.E., M.P.
Vice-President: Mr. Stanley H. Marshall, J.P.
Directors: R. I. Evans (Chairman), H. W. W. MacNaught (Vice-Chairman),
R. H. Hodgkiss, G. L. Richards, R. R. Wale,
H. De, F. O. Mound
Hon. Surgeon: Mr. H. De
Hon. Solicitor: Mr. H. W. W. MacNaught
Secretary/Manager: Mr. W. Jones

Photo by Mr. H. De

**A known and trusted service**
**throughout the British Isles . . .**
The history of Kay & Co. Ltd., established
in 1794, is one of rare achievement and
outstanding progress.
The energy and enterprise of the genera-
tions have built it into the largest Mail
Order Company in Europe and many hun-
dreds of people from Worcester and the
surrounding countryside are employed by
this Company, playing their part in an
organisation which supplies almost every
need of the British family.

## KAY & COMPANY LTD.
Worcester       Leeds       Glasgow
York     Newtown     Montgomeryshire

# COOPER & CO.
## WORCESTER'S PREMIER JEWELLERS

Excellent selection of High-Grade Watches
and Clocks, Engagement and Wedding
Rings always in stock

**Sports Cups and Tankards a Speciality**

Special Presentation Discounts

## 20 THE CROSS, WORCESTER
Tel.: 22514

# Loakes Park

◄

Programme from
Wycombe Wanderers v. Slough Town
11th August 1987

Programme from
Yeovil Town v. Swindon Town
11th May 1986

►►

Programme from
Yeovil Town v. Hastings United
13th February 1960

# Huish

# YEOVIL TOWN

## FOOTBALL CLUB

SEASON           1985 86

OFFICIAL
PROGRAMME

**30 pence**

| Match no. 27 | Friendly |
|---|---|
| **Swindon Town** | |
| Sunday, 11th May, 1986 | K.O. 5.00 p.m. |

VAUXHALL·OPEL

League

---

# YEOVIL TOWN
## FOOTBALL CLUB

Photo by W. H. Rendell, Yeovil

| No. 29 | Saturday, 13th February, 1960 |
|---|---|
| **HASTINGS** | |
| Southern League | Kick-off 3 p.m. |
| Next Home Match | Saturday, 20th February, 1960 |
| **BARNSTAPLE** | |
| Western League | Kick-off 3 p.m. |

OFFICIAL PROGRAMME    **4ᴰ**

*Issued by the*
YEOVIL TOWN FOOTBALL SUPPORTERS' CLUB

3783

EYEMOUTH UNITED F.C.

Kick-off 2.45    Souvenir Programme    Saturday, 26th January 1952

## SCOTTISH CUP
### FIRST ROUND

Photo : News Service, Berwick

## EYEMOUTH U. 6ᵈ
## EAST FIFE
VERSUS

# Playing Fields Park 182

◀

Programme from
Eyemouth United v. East Fife
26th January 1952

▶

Programme from
Fraserburgh v. Fort William
18th September 1999

# Bellslea Park

▶▶

Programme from
Gala Rovers v. John Collins All Stars 6th
August 2004

# Netherdale

# the Broch

### OFFICIAL MATCHDAY PROGRAMME

SCOTTISH QUALIFYING CUP (NORTH) 2nd ROUND

## FRASERBURGH

*versus*

## FORT WILLIAM

BELLSLEA PARK, FRASERBURGH

SATURDAY, 18th SEPTEMBER, 1999

### OFFICIAL PROGRAMME £1

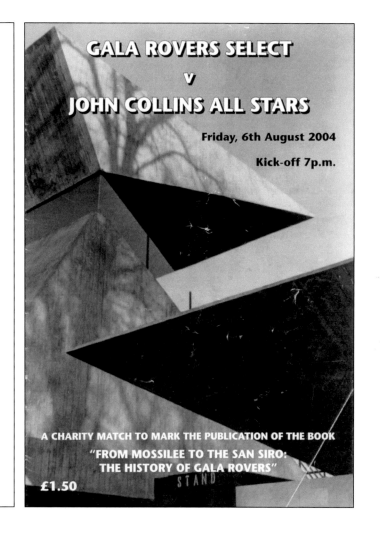

## GALA ROVERS SELECT
## v
## JOHN COLLINS ALL STARS

**Friday, 6th August 2004**

**Kick-off 7p.m.**

A CHARITY MATCH TO MARK THE PUBLICATION OF THE BOOK

"FROM MOSSILEE TO THE SAN SIRO:
THE HISTORY OF GALA ROVERS"

£1.50

# Hawick Royal Albert

Versus **TYNECASTLE**

Central Taxis East of Scotland League

Saturday 12th December 2015    Kick off: 2.00pm

At Netherdale 3G Arena, Galashiels

Programme No 79;  Minimum donation £1      Albert Park last weekend
www.hawickroyalalbert.co.uk               Picture courtesy of Fraser Hunter

# Albert Park

◄

Programme from
Hawick Royal Albert v. Tynecastle
12th December 2015

►

Programme from
Jeanfield Swifts v. Downfield
1st October 1988

# Simpson Park

►►

Programme from
Petershill v. Irvine Meadow
11th March 2006

# Petershill Park

# SWIFTS SCENE

**OFFICIAL PROGRAMME OF
JEANFIELD SWIFTS JUNIOR FOOTBALL CLUB**

SIMPSON PARK, CRIEFF ROAD,
PERTH

**20p**

# PETERSHILL F.C.
## Founded 1897

**PETERSHILL PARK     1935 - 2005**

OFFICIAL PROGRAMME 2005 - 2006
LUCKY NUMBER      N⁰ 2487

# Afan Lido
# Sports Ground

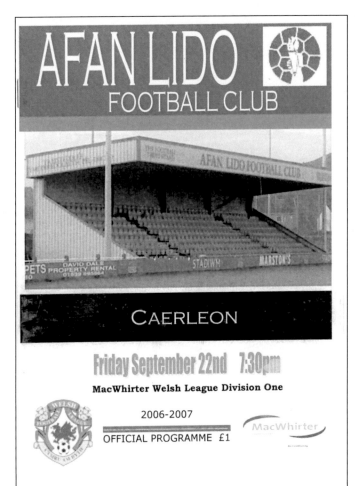

◀

Programme from
Afan Lido v. Caerleon
22nd September 2006

▶

Programme from
Bangor City v. Stafford Rangers
23rd April 1973

▶▶

Programme from
Bangor City v. Connah's Quay Nomads
1st September 1992

# Farrar Road

# Bangor City Football Club

### SEASON 1972-73

Chairman : T. G. Cowell     Vice-Chairman : Frank Wood
Sec./Treas. : Lal Jones, 39 Newton Street, Llanberis.     Tel. 335
Ground : Farrar Road, Bangor  . . . . . . .     Tel. 3015

NORTHERN PREMIER LEAGUE  —  BANGOR CITY

v.

## STAFFORD RANGERS

### Monday, 23rd April, 1973

*OFFICIAL PROGRAMME*

PRICE 4p            Kick-off 3.00 p.m.

*Clwb Pêldroed Dinas Bangor*

---

# Jenner Park

Photograph by Peter Wilson

**JENNER PARK, BARRY**

**ABACUS WELSH LEAGUE**
**NATIONAL DIVISION**

## BARRY TOWN

v

## EBBW VALE

**SATURDAY, 16th JANUARY, 1988**
**Kick-off 2.15 p.m.**
**Programme 30p**

Welsh Brewers Ltd

Barry Advertiser Ltd.

◀

Programme from
Barry Town v. Ebbw Vale
16th January 1988

▶

Programme from
Caernarfon Town v. Bangor City
29th January 1997

# The Oval

▶▶

Programme from
Caersws v. Llanelli
20th November 1993

# Recreation Ground

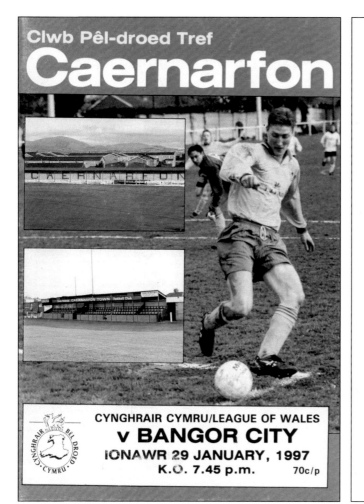

# Clwb Pêl-droed Tref
# Caernarfon

**CYNGHRAIR CYMRU/LEAGUE OF WALES**
## v BANGOR CITY
**IONAWR 29 JANUARY, 1997**
**K.O. 7.45 p.m.**      70c/p

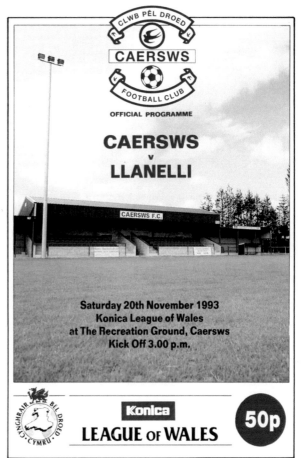

**CLWB PÊL DROED**
## CAERSWS
**FOOTBALL CLUB**

OFFICIAL PROGRAMME

## CAERSWS
v
## LLANELLI

CAERSWS F.C.

**Saturday 20th November 1993**
**Konica League of Wales**
**at The Recreation Ground, Caersws**
**Kick Off 3.00 p.m.**

**Konica**
## LEAGUE OF WALES

50p

Official
Programme
30p

# Recreation Field

◄

Programme from
Carno v. Worcester City
31st August 1990

▶

Programme from
Goytre United v. Pontyclun
6th October 2012

# Glenhafod Park

▶▶

Programme from
Haverfordwest County v. Caersws
17th April 1999

# Bridge Meadow

## Welcome to Glenhafod Park Stadium
Home of Goytre United Football Club – Season 2012 -13
McWhirter Welsh League – Division 1

# Goytre United AFC

### A PROUD HISTORY A GREAT FUTURE

Welsh League Division One Champions 2005/06, 2007/08, 2009/10
Welsh League Cup Winners 2004/05, 2007/08

**GB**vehicle
**contracts**
OFFICIAL SHIRT SPONSOR

**OFFICIAL MATCH PROGRAMME**
**£1.00**

---

MAIN SPONSORS
**CALDER**
OFFICE SUPPLIES

*The Bluebirds*

# HAVERFORDWEST
# COUNTY AFC

### The Bridge Meadow Stadium

**£1.00**
Official Matchday Programme

FOOTBALL LEAGUE OF WALES

**1998/99**

◀

Programme from
Holywell Town v. Porthmadog
25th March 2003

▶

Programme from
Llanidloes Town v. Aberystwyth Town
24th April 1993

# Victoria Avenue

# Llanidloes Town F.C.

**THE FOOTBALL LEAGUE OF WALES**

Inter CableTel F.C.
v
Ebbw Vale

THE FOOTBALL
LEAGUE of WALES

Photo: Courtesy of South Wales Echo

## Welcome to
## CARDIFF ATHLETIC STADIUM
### Season 1996/97

• TUESDAY 3rd SEPTEMBER 1996 •
K.O. 7.30pm

# Cardiff Athletics Stadium

◀

Programme from
Inter CableTel v. Ebbw Vale
3rd September 1996

▶

Programme from
Llansantffraid v. Holywell Town
2 January 1995

# Recreation Ground

▶▶

Programme from
Merthyr Tydfil v. Dover Athletic
27th August 1994

# Penydarren Park

## Llansantffraid Football Club

**Official Programme 1994/95**

# THE SAINT

**50p**

### LLANSANTFFRAID
Vs
**HOLYWELL TOWN**
Monday, 2nd January, 1995

**LEAGUE OF WALES**

THE FOOTBALL
LEAGUE of WALES

---

**Official Programme**
**1994-1995**

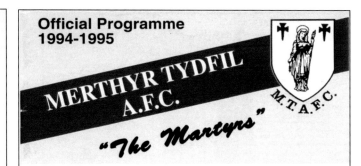

# MERTHYR TYDFIL A.F.C.

*"The Martyrs"*

**M.T.A.F.C.**

VAUXHALL
CONFERENCE

Main Sponsors
**HOOVER**

**GM Vauxhall Conference Saturday August 27th 1994 Kick Off 3.00pm**

### Penydarren Park, Merthyr Tydfil

V

# DOVER ATHLETIC

**Issue No. 2**

**£1.00**

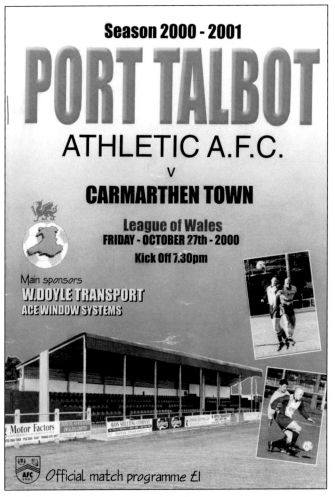

# Victoria Road

◄

Programme from
Port Talbot Athletic v. Carmarthen Town
27th October 2000

►►

Programme from
Newport AFC v. Ilkeston Town
27th March 1996

# Newport Stadium

# THE Exile

### The Official Match Magazine and Voice of

# NEWPORT AFC

NEWPORT A.F.C.
THE EXILES
FOUNDED JUNE 1989

Beazer Homes League

NEWPORT STADIUM

**FOOTBALL WITH A FUTURE**

| Beazer Homes League Premier Division £1.20 1995 - 1996 | Match Sponsors Courage | ILKESTON TOWN Wed 27th March 1996 KO 7.45 pm |

# Latham Park

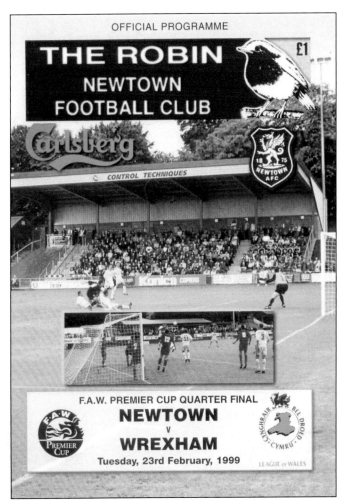

◀
Programme from
Newtown v. Wrexham
23rd February 1999

▶
Programme from
Newtown v. Caersws
3rd September 1994

▶▶
Programme from
Newtown v. Accrington Stanley
16th March 1991

# Latham Park

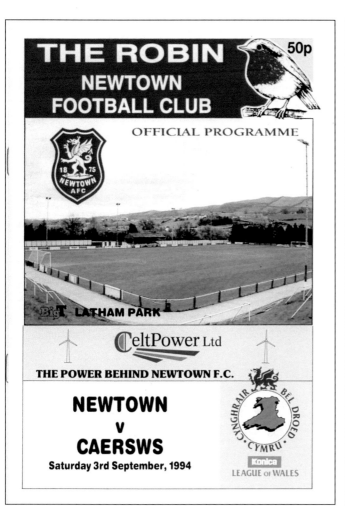

# THE ROBIN

## NEWTOWN FOOTBALL CLUB

### OFFICIAL PROGRAMME

50p

**BigT LATHAM PARK**

**CeltPower Ltd**

**THE POWER BEHIND NEWTOWN F.C.**

## NEWTOWN
### v
## CAERSWS

**Saturday 3rd September, 1994**

CYNGHRAIR BEL DROED CYMRU

Konica

LEAGUE of WALES

# THE ROBIN

## NEWTOWN FOOTBALL CLUB

30p

## NEWTOWN
### v.
## ACCRINGTON STANLEY

**Saturday 16th March, 1991**

K.O. 3.00 p.m.

**HFS LOANS LEAGUE**

BWRDD DATBLYGU CYMRU WLEDIG DEVELOPMENT BOARD FOR RURAL WALES

# Ponciau Park

◄

Programme from
Rhos Aelwyd v. Oswestry
2nd April 1996

**CLWB PÊLDROED**
**RHOS AELWYD**
**FOOTBALL CLUB**
*Ground - Ponciau Park, Rhosllannerchrugog*
*Season 1995 - 96*
*Official Programme*

**SPONSORED BY**
**TAN Y CLAWDD MOTORS LTD**
**M & E CARTWRIGHT**
*TRAWLER FISH BAR*

►

Programme from
Rhyl v. Penrhyncoch
12th March 2011

►►

Programme from
Rhyl v. Haverfordwest County
6th September 1999

# Belle Vue

£1:50

# rhyl fc

Official Matchday Programme / Rhaglen Swyddogol

Season 2010 - 11

**MATCH SPONSOR**
**MICHAEL PHILLIPS**
**CARE AGENCY**

Huws Gray Alliance
**RHYL FC**
vs
**PENRHYNCOCH**
**Saturday 12th March 2011**

## Croeso I Clwb Pel Droed Y Rhyl

# RHYL FOOTBALL CLUB

OFFICIAL PROGRAMME/RHAGLEN SWYDDOGOL
SEASON/TYMOR 1998/99          PRICE £1.00

CLUB SPONSORS
## uhlsport

SATURDAY MARCH 6TH 1999
RHYL
V
HAVERFORDWEST COUNTY
(Football League of Wales - Kick Off 2.30pm)

## CLWB PEL-DROED Y RHYL

# Rhayader

# Football Club

**Season 1992/1993**

Official Programme 30p

## The Weirglodd

◄

Programme from
Rhayader v. Carno
12th September 1992

►

Programme from
Tredegar Town v. Caerleon
11th September 2004

# Tredegar Leisure Complex

# *Tredegar Town AFC*

Today's Match Sponsor
Noel Harris

SATURDAY 11TH SEPTEMBER 2004 - KICK OFF 2.30PM
WELSH SENIOR CUP 1ST ROUND
v **CAERLEON**

**MOTAQUOTE WELSH LEAGUE DIVISION 2 - SEASON 2004/05**

# Ynys Park

◀

Programme from
Ton Pentre v. Barry Town
8th October 1988

▶

Programme from
Welshpool Town v. Flint Town United
15th March 2000

▶▶

Programme from
Welshpool Town v. Llansantffraid Village
27th August 2012

# Maesydre

# WELSHPOOL TOWN F.C.

HUWS GRAY - FITLOCK CYMRU ALLIANCE

v

## FLINT TOWN UNITED

### Wednesday, 15th March, 2000

50p

# Welshpool Town FC

## v Llansantffraid Village

### Programme £1 – Kick Off 11.00am

BARCHESTER
*Celebrating life*

SPAR Spar Mid Wales League Division 1

# Index